Russia in the Eighteenth Century

Russia in the Eighteenth Century

FROM PETER THE GREAT TO CATHERINE THE GREAT

(1696–1796)

A. LENTIN

Associate Professor of History
University of Waterloo, Ontario

BOOKS
10 East 53d St., New York 10022
(a division of Harper & Row Publishers, Inc.)

Published in the U.S.A. 1973 by
Harper & Row Publishers, Inc.
Barnes & Noble Import Division

PREFACE

'To imagine 18th-century Europe without Russia is impossible',[*] observes Professor Barraclough. Professor Beloff echoes the sentiment, discerning in Russia's emergence as a Great Power nothing less than 'the major development of the whole century'.[†] Yet for the student, sixth-former or general reader with an interest in 18th-century Russia— (whether for its own sake or as a background to the reigns of Paul and Alexander I and the Napoleonic and Decembrist experiences)—there is little available by way of a brief introductory survey. The present short synopsis attempts, without assuming previous specialized knowledge, to outline some of the more significant features of Russian history from Peter I to Catherine II. Of necessity much has been omitted. In considering the subject primarily from the standpoint of 'westernization', I have, to take but one example, barely hinted at the problems confronting Russia as a multi-national empire. The reader will doubtless single out other topics which have likewise received scant attention. Should he or she be tempted (or provoked) into exploring these and other aspects at greater length, and, hopefully, to probe some of the sources and secondary studies listed in the bibliography, the book will have served its purpose. My thanks to John Keep, who suggested the idea of the book and to Ruth Laser for her help with the maps.

A. Lentin
Linton, Cambridgeshire, 1973

[*] G. Barraclough, *History in a Changing World* (Oxford, 1956), p. 193.
[†] M. Beloff, *The Age of Absolutism 1660–815* (London, 1967), p. 43.

To Professor Elizabeth Hill
in appreciation

CONTENTS

PREFACE   v

PART I
THE AGE OF PETER THE GREAT
1696–1725

1 Resurgence   3
2 'A Regulated State'   14
3 A Nation in Harness   24
4 Education and 'Westernization'   36

PART II
MID-CENTURY RUSSIA
1725–1762

5 The Age of 'Palace-Revolutions'   47
6 Russia as a European Power   61
7 The Rise of the Nobility   68
8 St. Petersburg Culture   72

PART III
THE AGE OF CATHERINE THE GREAT
1762–1796

9 Catherine II and 'Enlightened Absolutism'   79
10 Action Abroad   93
11 The 'Golden Age' of the Nobility   99
12 The Russian Enlightenment   110
SUGGESTIONS FOR FURTHER READING   125
INDEX   123

LIST OF PLATES

I   Bronze bust of Peter the Great   *between pages 24 and 25*
II   The Twelve Colleges, St. Petersburg
III The Admiralty, St. Petersburg

IV   Forge   *between pages 40 and 41*
V   Peter the Great
VI   Menshikov
VII Empress Anna
VIII Empress Elizabeth
IX   Pyotr Shuvalov

X   Catherine the Great   *between pages 80 and 81*
XI   The Battle of Chesme
XII Catherine II celebrates the victory of Chesme
XIII The Gibbet
XIV Portrait of Pugachov superimposed on a portrait of
       Catherine II
XV   Nicholas Ivanovitch Novikov
XVI Beggars
XVII Mademoiselle Nelidova

LIST OF MAPS

1. Russia's westward expansion under Peter I (the shaded area represents Russia's acquisitions by the Treaty of Nystadt 1721)   *page 2*

2. Russia and the Seven Years' War   *page 46*

3. Russia's westward expansion under Catherine II and the course of the Pugachov rebellion   *page 78*

I
THE AGE OF PETER
THE GREAT
1696-1725

1. Russia's westward expansion under Peter I, The shaded area represents Russia's acquisitions by the Treaty of Mystadt, 1721.

I

Resurgence

Muscovy and Isolationism

Toward the end of the seventeenth century, Russia was starting to emerge from an isolation so chronic and deep-seated that it was difficult for other Europeans to think of her as part of their world. Since the 1580s, while western Europe surged ahead with unprecedented vigour, Russia lagged far behind. Her contact with the west was limited; indeed she was barred from normal relations by a cordon of hostile neighbours, Sweden, Poland and Turkey, each occupying large tracts of her territory and blocking her access to the Baltic and Black Sea. Russia, geographically a super-power, by far the largest state in Europe (to say nothing of Asia) was, observed Descartes in 1648, of less weight in European affairs than the minutest German principality. His paradox was not without point: so little was Russia known in the west that in 1657 Louis XIV wrote to Czar Michael, unaware that his addressee had been dead a dozen years.

How had this come about? For most of the seventeenth century, Russia, or the Grand Duchy of Muscovy, as it was called, was struggling to recover from her sudden and disastrous decline during the 'Time of Troubles' (1584–1613). After dynamic, westward-oriented rule in the fifteenth and sixteenth centuries, she had, with the expiry of the reigning dynasty, fallen prey to internal anarchy and foreign aggression. Torn by dynastic feuds, boyar *frondes* and peasant uprisings, she laid herself open to invasion by Poland and Sweden, who took advantage of her weakness to wrench away whole provinces in the north and west. Moscow itself fell into Polish hands, and successive Polish usurpers occupied the throne of the czars, to the immense indignation of the people. At last, by a supreme national effort which savoured much of a crusade, the foreigners were expelled from Moscow and the Romanov dynasty was elected to rule as autocrats.

All that Russians seemed to want now was peace and quiet. After recent experience, few were enamoured of the west. The moral of the 'Time of Troubles' seemed to be that Russia should henceforth turn in upon herself and have no more truck with foreigners.

Distrust of the west was fanned by religion. The Orthodox Church fostered the notion of Moscow as the 'Third Rome', sole heir to Rome and Constantinople, and the only true and undefiled repository of Christianity; and condemned the religious heterodoxy of the west as heathendom. Together with this went a sweeping aversion for western society and culture, a refusal to accept that foreign examples might be advantageous, and a complacent certainty that 'Holy Russia' had nothing to learn from outsiders. While Ivan IV* had readily adopted western methods, seventeenth-century Russia preferred on the whole to turn her back on the rest of Europe. To display the slightest partiality for western customs was to invite stiff opposition: attempts to introduce foreign dress or theatrical entertainments at court invariably brought down anathemas from the Patriarch. If the Church was so set against these superficial trappings of western life, its attitude towards serious westernization was still more unyielding.

It opposed rationalism. It was not just that Russia was virtually untouched by the great civilizing tides that had swept across the west— the Renaissance, the Reformation, the advent of the Scientific Spirit; rather she had no wish to know of them: she gloried in her ignorance, despising secular knowledge as the work of Satan. 'If ye are asked'— so ran a precept of the time—'"Do ye know philosophy?" ye shall reply: "I have not practiced Greek subtleties, nor read eloquent astronomers, nor conversed with wise philosophers. I have read the books of God's Law, if haply my sinful soul may be cleansed of its sins."' When, in order to counter the work of Polish Jesuit missions in the Ukraine, the Church founded her own theological academy at Kiev in 1631, its methods were based not on the humanistic rationalism of the Renaissance but on the scholasticism of the Middle Ages. And when the Church attempted to introduce marginal reforms in ritual and liturgy, so strong was popular feeling against any tampering with traditional rites, that the Church was split asunder in the great Schism of 1667. Tens of thousands of so-called Old Believers broke away from

*Ivan the Terrible, ruled 1547–84.

the mother church, choosing to flee into the forests or to suffer martyr-
dom by self-immolation, rather than make the sign of the cross with
three fingers instead of two, or make four genuflections instead of
twelve during a certain prayer.

Not content with the last word on faith and worship, the Church
also claimed authority in matters of state. Its prestige was impressive:
at the election of a Patriarch, it was customary for the Czar to prostrate
himself in symbolic obeisance at the feet of the new incumbent. In the
1620s Patriarch Filaret was proclaimed co-ruler of Russia with young
Czar Michael, enjoying the title 'Great Sovereign'. Later, Patriarch
Nikon assumed supreme power during Czar Alexei's absence in the
field. True, Nikon's political pretensions proved so overweening that
even the notoriously mild and pious Alexei removed him from office
and clipped the Church's wings by pronouncing the separation of
Church and state (1667).

Yet blows at the authority of the Church did nothing to shake the
authority of religion itself or its pervasive hold on men's minds.
Though Russians differed over forms and rituals and disputed the
extent of the Church's political power, they seldom dreamed of
questioning the spiritual premises of Orthodoxy, or denying the overriding necessity of personal salvation. Life outside a framework of piety
and devotion was unthinkable.

Seventeenth-century czars were worried by the effects of this
spiritual exclusiveness on Russia's political position. They recognized
that isolationism, deeply attractive though it was, would defeat its own
ends: unless Russia was prepared to keep pace with the west—which
meant taking lessons from the Europeans—she would lay herself permanently open to aggression. But in order to gain closer contact with
the west, she must first break the stranglehold of Sweden, Poland and
Turkey; and to do this she must remedy her military backwardness.
To this end various measures were taken: an armament-works under
Dutch management was founded at Tula in 1632; and foreign mercenaries were invited to Russia to remodel her armies and demonstrate
western firearms. The *Strel'tsy*, a trained body of regulars under
Swedish and German officers, was set up at Moscow. But the foreigners,
so essential to Russia's recovery, were received by the people and the
Church with sullen suspicion and hostility. For fear of spiritual contami-
nation and for their own physical safety they were confined to a special
ghetto in Moscow, the so-called 'German Quarter'.

Such attempts at westernization were less than whole-hearted, and their results were disappointing. Under Czar Michael (1613–1645) there were two wars with Poland and one with Sweden; all three ended disastrously. Under Alexei (1645–1676) there followed another two wars with Poland, ending in a compromise peace in 1667, and another ill-fated war with Sweden. Under Czar Fyodor (1676–1682) and the Regent Sofia (1682–1689), Russia, in her first European coalition, joined Poland and Austria against Turkey. The outcome, however, was two successive disasters in the south (1687 and 1698). In three-quarters of a century of intermittent war, Russia regained Smolensk, Kiev and Malorussia from the Poles, but made no headway against the Swedes, who still held the road to the Baltic; or the Turks, who, through their vassals the Crimean Tartars, blocked the path to the Black Sea. Russia's only maritime contact with Europe was via the North-West Passage from the White Sea port of Archangel, icebound for half the year.

Peter I and the Challenge of Modernity

In 1696 Peter I assumed sole rule at the age of twenty-four. A new, more vigorous tempo was introduced in the process of modernization. Unlike his predecessors, Peter had grown up in the company of foreigners in the 'German Quarter'. Here, smoking, drinking, and roistering with German, Scots and Dutch artisans, he developed a passion for western ways and western technology.

Peter was both the agent and symbol of change. Physically a giant, well over six feet tall, with matching strength and breadth of stride, he was above all a man of action. Manual crafts of every kind enthralled him: already in his twenties he was a master carpenter, shipwright and bombardier. He could never stand by and watch others work without lending a hand himself; and his mind operated on the material and mechanical plane. Peter was a rough, outdoor man with hearty animal tastes; bluff and direct, he lacked refinement and compassion. Typically, in his impatience with tradition, he threw off his first wife (the match was an arranged one, as was customary in Muscovy), and lived openly with a young Livonian serving-maid, whom he later made his wife and empress. People to him were little more than cogs in a machine, functional and expendable; in his fervour for change he spared no one, himself least of all. He believed that his subjects had to be bludgeoned into action: only the result mattered, not the cost. It was clear to him that success in Russian foreign policy could come only from more direct and uninhibited contact with the west. Any contrary notions he swept aside with angry scorn. He despised isolationism, flouted traditional taboos, mocked the Church's fulminations and rode roughshod over hallowed custom.

Peter's first foreign commitment was to the coalition against Turkey. An assault on the fort of Azov in 1695 had miscarried. The Turks controlled the Black Sea and could supply the fort unmolested. Peter determined to challenge their dominion at sea. Experts were hurriedly summoned from the west to direct the construction of a galley-fleet, and the next year saw a second attempt on Azov. This time, the Turks, besieged both by land and sea, were forced to surrender, ceding the ports of Azov and Taganrog. A triumphal march through Moscow celebrated Russia's first naval victory.

Another novelty was Peter's embassy to the west (1697–99). Never before had a czar ventured outside Muscovy. Peter's mission was partly diplomatic, an attempt to bolster up the coalition. But it also arose from sheer curiosity, the desire to see more of the superior techniques which he had admired in the German Quarter. Characteristic of his urge to learn was his apprenticeship at a Dutch shipyard. He was not disappointed with his experiences: the crowded docks and arsenals of Amsterdam and Portsmouth confirmed his conviction of Russia's chronic backwardness and the need for Russia too to undergo her apprenticeship. Strengthened, too, was his resolve to give expression to Russia's long pent-up resources of manpower and material in terms of political influence and the prestige of Great Power status.

The Struggle with Sweden 1700–1709

War with Turkey had brought Russia a measure of success which seemed to auger further triumphs in the south. But Peter saw a prospect of easier gains in the north. By 1700 Sweden seemed on the edge of decline, her treasury depleted, her nobility disaffected, her tiny population clinging to possessions on the Russian side of the Baltic which seemed beyond her capacity to retain. Now surely the time was ripe to dislodge her from this foothold and put an end to her domination of the north. Hastily making peace with Turkey, and allying himself with Denmark and Saxony-Poland, Peter declared war on Sweden (1700).

Appearances were deceptive. Peter, as he admitted, had blundered into hostilities without forethought or preparation. The meteoric young Charles XII of Sweden darted up with astounding verve, to set his enemies reeling on every side. Within months, he knocked Denmark out of the war, thrust the Saxons back from Riga, and, in a lightning dash across the Baltic with a mere 8,000 men, defeated a Russian army of 35,000 at Narva. The Russians, raw and undisciplined, fled in panic, leaving their entire artillery and scores of their foreign officers in enemy hands. Sweden's reputation soared, while Russia was discounted in the chanceries of the west. Peter wept in the bitterness of defeat. His position was grave indeed. Had Charles followed up his victory by advancing on Moscow, Peter would have been hard put to stop him. But Charles, always over-contemptuous of his opponents, left Russia in peace for the moment to concentrate on Saxony-Poland. This gave Peter a valuable breathing-space in which to take stock of his position and make good his losses.

Russia had lost a battle, not a war. Narva was only the first round in a struggle that was to drag itself out for twenty-one years. Swiftly recovering from his initial despair, Peter showed himself quite undaunted and ready to begin again. This was one of the characteristics of his greatness. He lacked the spectacular flair or the personal magnetism of Charles. But he had the qualities that ultimately brought complete success: boundless energy and resilience, realism, singlemindedness and enterprise, the ability to learn from his mistakes, to husband his resources, to await the opportune moment and to strike only after long and thorough preparation. 'I know the Swedes will long continue to be victorious,' he said, 'but in time they will teach us to beat them.'

Accepting that without complete reorganization his troops were no match for the Swedes, he at once set about forging Russia's vastly superior but fatally under-organized resources into an effective war-machine. The whole nation was harnessed to the task of military reform, all other considerations taking second place. Journeying the length and breadth of the Empire, Peter enforced his will with an iron hand and at a feverish pace, preparing to resume the conflict on more equal terms. Such was his sense of urgency that he ordered church-bells to be melted down for armaments to replace his lost artillery. Peter himself readily turned a hand to every task, from recruiting and drilling to shipbuilding, mineral prospecting and iron-smelting, demonstrating, as he said, that 'his hands were as horny as any of his subjects'.

While seventeenth-century czars had borrowed desultorily from the west, Peter's borrowings were on a massive scale and at a much accelerated pace. He believed that his only hope of saving Russia from imminent and total defeat by Sweden lay in the immediate application of modern methods, direct from Europe. A general proclamation to the west in 1702 offered high salaries to foreign experts willing to settle in Russia and help hew her army into shape. A flood of instructors poured into the country, bringing new weapons, drills, tactics and techniques. Among the most important of these innovations was the latest achievement of western gunnery—the flintlock and bayonet—which the Russian infantry was soon to put to good use as an offensive weapon. Factories were set up to supply guns, ammunition and uniforms. To replace the haphazard combination of volunteer mercenaries and peasant levies on which Russia had depended hitherto, Peter imposed compulsory mass conscription. Russia became a nation under arms.

Meanwhile, Charles XII was wearing down Polish resistance. Peter, while sending his tottering ally what help he could spare, was slowly edging the isolated Swedish garrisons out of the Baltic provinces and gaining a foothold on the Gulf of Finland. Gradually, his forces in this area gained the upper hand, acquiring renewed skill and confidence with each successful operation. Once established on the Gulf, Peter set about building a Baltic fleet to be used in conjunction with his army. In 1703, on the marshy Neva estuary, he laid the foundations of his new capital, St Petersburg, and in 1704, avenged his initial defeat by capturing Narva.

But his position was far from secure. In 1707, Poland was knocked out of the war. Russia, alone and without allies, faced the most powerful army in northern Europe, its leader at the height of his career. On the outcome of this confrontation depended Russia's entry into the modern world. Peter's position was endangered by a series of internal uprisings. No sooner had he suppressed a revolt in Astrakhan, than insurrection sprang up among the Don Cossacks, while among the Bashkirs of the Urals rebellion was endemic. Peter had to divert much-needed forces to suppress these local outbreaks, while preparing to confront the Swedes, who in 1708, struck out across the Russian frontier with an army of 45,000.

Cautiously, the Russians withdrew, enticing the Swedes to follow into the interior and destroying the supplies in their path. They deliberately avoided open battle in favour of timely raids on the Swedish communications. Near the village of Lesnaya, 14,000 men under Peter and Sheremetev ambushed a Swedish supply-convoy, putting 16,000 troops to flight. This was a cheering victory. Not only had Peter deprived Charles of much-needed reinforcements, but his troops had proved that they had the training and stamina to take on a first-class army.

At this juncture, Charles committed what was to prove a fatal error. Abandoning his plan for a direct advance on Moscow, he resolved to join forces with the Ukrainian hetman Mazepa, who had undertaken to rally the Ukraine to his side. Marching far into southern Malorussia, with inadequate supplies and ever-lengthening lines of communication, he wintered in inhospitable country. For although Mazepa joined him with a token force, the Ukraine as a whole refused to throw in its lot with the Swedes.

Peter took full advantage of the Swedes' discomfiture. When, in the summer of 1709, Charles laid siege to the small fortress of Poltava, three armies under Peter, Menshikov, and Sheremetev converged upon him, cutting off his retreat. A fresh and well-equipped Russian force of 40,000 faced 30,000 tired and dispirited Swedes, weak with sickness and lack of food. Charles himself had been wounded and entrusted his command to Field-Marshal Rehnsköld. When battle was joined on June 27, the Swedish army was annihilated. Rehnsköld fell in battle, Charles and Mazepa fled to Turkey, and several Swedish generals were captured.

Poltava was a vindication of the years of hard training. No longer an undisciplined rabble, the Russian forces now constituted a seasoned European army. Toasting the captured Swedish generals after the battle, Peter drank to the health of 'our masters', who had taught Russia to realize her own prowess.

Birth of the Russian Empire 1709–1725

Poltava marks the decisive turning-point in the war. With the destruction of Charles' main army, Russia was free from the threat of defeat, and although the war was to drag on for another twelve years, Sweden's hegemony of the north was lost forever. The victory revived the coalition with Denmark and Saxony and gave Russia a dominant voice in Polish affairs. Statesmen in the west had viewed Peter's early failures with derision; after Poltava, their attitude changed to respect or alarm, as Peter set about gathering the fruits of victory. In 1710 the Russians took final possession of Livonia and Estonia, and strengthened their hold on Ingria with the capture of Vyborg, the 'bolster' of St Petersburg.

Peter's gains were suddenly imperilled by a disastrous turn of events in the south. The Turks, never reconciled to the loss of Azov and Taganrog, and urged on at Constantinople by Charles, declared war in 1710. Hurrying south the following year, Peter advanced deep into Moldavia, counting on an uprising of the Balkan Christians which failed to materialize. Hemmed in on the river Pruth near Stanileshti by a Turkish army three times greater than his own, he was forced to sue for peace. Total ruin seemed inevitable: Peter even steeled himself to the necessity of surrendering his Baltic conquests. Thanks partly to the diplomatic skill of his envoy Shafirov, no such sacrifice was needed. The Turks were satisfied with the surrender of Azov and Taganrog, and the dismantling of the Azov galley-fleet. Even so, the terms were bad enough, and hopes of a foothold on the Black Sea had to be postponed indefinitely.

In the north, the war continued to turn slowly in Russia's favour. Peter urgently needed to enlarge his Baltic fleet. As well as relying on his new dockyards at St Petersburg, he bought up a quantity of old warships from England, Holland and France. With these, and more especially with a new fleet of light, manoeuvrable galleys, he began to challenge Sweden's hegemony at sea. In 1714, the Russians encountered the Swedish fleet off Cape Hango. Immobilized by a sudden calm, the enemy vessels lay at the mercy of the galleys, which picked them off at leisure one by one. As a result of this lucky triumph, the whole of Finland fell under Russian control, together with Abo and the Aaland Islands, from where raids were mounted against the Swedish mainland. By 1725, Russian naval supremacy in the Baltic was firmly established, with a warfleet of nearly 50 battleships as well as 400 galleys and smaller vessels.

The character of the war was transformed. From a more-or-less localized struggle between Russia and Sweden it became part of a wider, more intricate international chess-game. With the ending of the War of the Spanish Succession in the west, the whole of Europe turned its attention to the north, and Russia became almost as dependent on her diplomats as on her armies.

By 1716, her front line had advanced into Mecklenburg and was investing the Swedish possessions in northern Germany. This progress to the Elbe, into the heart of Europe, sent a tremor of alarm across the continent. The Russian presence added a new dimension to the accepted idea of the Balance of Power. In a second trip to the west in 1717, Peter urged a sensational scheme upon the French: Russia should take the place of Sweden, France's traditional ally in the north; together they would form an unbeatable alliance. Though France declined the offer as chimaeric, the fact that it could be made at all showed how far Russia's international position had advanced since 1700. To George I of England, Peter's growing influence in Germany seemed a threat to his Hanoverian possessions. A succession of British squadrons was despatched to the Baltic in 1719, 1720, and 1721, to try and revive Swedish resistance, which had flagged notably since the untimely death of Charles XII in 1718. At the Aaland peace-conference, the Swedes rejected Peter's terms and procrastinated, in the hope of further British support. But Peter, confident of his overpowering strength, intensified the pressure by multiplying his galley raids on the Swedish coast. These culminated in a descent near Stockholm itself. At last, in 1721, Sweden was forced to recognize the futility of further resistance. By the Treaty of Nystadt she surrendered Livonia, Estonia, Ingria and part of Karelia, yielding to Russia the outlets essential to her contact with the west. Russia now replaced Sweden as the dominant power in the north. Poland, devastated and exhausted, relapsed to the status of a Russian satellite. As early as 1710, Peter had contemplated her dismemberment. On the Baltic seaboard and in central Europe, Russian prestige was extended by a chain of minor German client-states, Courland, Mecklenburg and Holstein, each linked by marriage to the house of Romanov. Russian influence was also strong in Denmark and Prussia. At Peter's accession, Russia had only one permanent diplomatic mission in the west; by 1721 there were over twenty.

Behind the diplomats stood the army, one of the largest and most formidable in Europe. 200,000 regulars and 100,000 reserves stood permanently poised for action. Indeed, having dealt with Sweden, Peter at once sought out fresh conquests. In 1722, he invaded Persia, annexing several provinces and extending protection to Georgia and Armenia. In Siberia, his troops overran Semipalatinsk; and in the Far East annexed Kamchatka and the Kurile Islands.

In 1721, in celebration of the peace of Nystadt, Peter was proclaimed

'Emperor of all the Russias', a symbolic improvement on the former title 'Czar of Muscovy'; and received the accolade 'Peter the Great'. While Europe showed some hesitation in acknowledging his imperial title, she was less slow to accept the altered balance of power. Austria, France, Spain, and Sweden herself courted Russian favour. Even Turkey signed a treaty of friendship. Peter might certainly boast of having achieved 'an increase in Russia's glory'. Claiming by his Baltic conquests to have completed the task begun by Ivan IV, he declared that after her thirty-year apprenticeship, no country in Europe was so much feared as Russia. Certainly, his achievement was remarkable. In a quarter of a century of uninterrupted warfare, Russia had fought her way out of the encirclement and isolationism of the seventeenth century to find herself one of the Great Powers.

2

'A Regulated State'

The changes wrought by Peter between 1700 and 1709 stemmed, not from some carefully laid master-plan, but from the immediate exigencies of war, a cascade of stop-gap measures, hasty, tentative, often clumsy, adopted from day-to-day in the throes of a desperate struggle. After the debacle at Narva, Peter had no thought beyond staving off total collapse, and gradually, painfully, bringing about recovery. Only after Poltava, with the threat of defeat overcome, was there time for deliberate and consistent planning on peacetime lines; time, as Peter put it, to give Russia 'good and solid institutions' and make her 'a regulated state'. But Peter was a soldier above all; of the thirty years of his reign only one, 1724, was free from war, and long after Poltava, military thinking set the tone of government.

Senate and Colleges

Peter's continual absence from the seat of government raised a serious problem of continuity. In 1711, on leaving for the Pruth campaign, he created the Senate, a council of nine, to rule in his stead, and on his return, established it on a permanent basis as supreme executive council. As distinct from the Muscovite Boyars' Duma, which had claimed to govern in partnership with the Czar, the Senate was strictly subordinate to him; it was staffed by his nominees; its decisions became law only with his approval. One of its main functions was to raise funds: 'Money', as Peter put it, 'is the artery of war'. But it was also the nerve-centre of the bureaucracy: it supervised, directed and co-ordinated every branch of government: it gathered in the taxes, controlled the distribution of revenue, arranged the allocation of official posts; it promoted industry, trade, and education. It oversaw the smooth running of the administration in general. Lastly it functioned as supreme court of justice.

The Senate's chief institutional role was as a bureau for the formulation and execution of imperial policies. To ensure its efficiency Peter kept it under close scrutiny. Its sessions were attended by a Guards officer, with orders to arrest any senator whose conduct he thought divisive or time-wasting. In 1722, Peter created the office of Procurator-General, to act, in Peter's words, as 'the Czar's eye', and appointed to it the sharp-witted Yaguzhinsky. The Procurator-General attended the Senate's meetings, drew up its agenda and regulated the length of its debates. He could interrupt its proceedings and force it to reconsider resolutions of which he disapproved. He could even impose fines for an 'incorrect decision'. The Procurator-General's authority also extended beyond the Senate to cover the administration throughout the country at every level. Aided by a staff of procurators, he was empowered to intervene at will in order to rectify abuses and punish those responsible. After the Czar, to whom alone he was responsible, the Procurator-General was the most powerful official in Russia.

As long as the war dragged on, Peter had little time to reform the complex and cumbersome chancellery-system which he inherited from Muscovy. There were some fifty chancelleries or *prikazy*, their functions ill-defined and often overlapping, their procedures confused, arbitrary and slow. Peter tried to cut through this tangle by fits and starts. He amalgamated some chancelleries, abolished others, or set up new ones, according to the need of the moment. At one time he thought of replacing all chancelleries by an enlarged, all-embracing Senate. A final solution came in 1718, when, after consulting with western advisers (notably, Leibniz), he decided to remodel his administration on the collegiate principle prevalent in Germany and Scandinavia He abolished most of the chancelleries outright, reallocating the business of government into nine (later twelve) clear and separate categories, each the responsibility of a special board, or College. Three of the Colleges took charge of foreign policy and defence (the Colleges of Foreign Affairs, War, and the Admiralty). Three Colleges controlled finances (tax collection, revenue distribution, and payment of official salaries). Other Colleges supervised trade, commerce and industry. Finally, there was a College of Justice.

This distribution of functions reflects the overriding priority given to military needs. Of the nine main Colleges, three were concerned with war and diplomacy—(and the authority of these 'first three Colleges' was always paramount); and six with maintaining the war effort on the home front. If the Senate was the hub of government, the Colleges were the spokes linking it to the day-to-day execution of orders. General directives from the Senate were translated by the Colleges into practical measures, and passed on to the provincial authorities. These, in turn, reported back through the Colleges to the Senate. Each College was run by a president, a vice-president (usually a foreign expert) and a committee of eight or nine; and each had its own chancery or secretariat to deal with paper-work. In both Senate and Colleges, decisions were reached by majority vote. Detailed rules of procedure were laid down in the *General Regulation* of 1720.

Peter had high hopes of his Senate and Colleges as paragons of rational modern government. But their machinery did not always work with the clockwork precision predicted by Leibniz. The problem of liaison between the Colleges and the provinces became chronic. To some degree this was unavoidable in a country as vast as Russia, where it took time to collate information and forward it to the capital. But it meant that, for example, the Colleges responsible for finance were without adequate statistical information for two years after their opening. Inevitable teething-troubles arose from switching over from the familiar and looser chancellery system. Because of the new regulations, a given problem took several weeks at least to be resolved; and procrastination and squabbling were commonplace, as president vied with vice-president and Russian with foreigner.

Impatient with delays and incompetence, Peter tended to undermine his own collegiate principle by relying on individual henchmen, whom he consulted outside their official frame of reference. He found a tight inner council of personal supporters to be the most effective executive machine. In addition, he strengthened the powers of his watchdogs. To supplement the Procurator-General and his staff he created a network of *fiskals*, or secret government agents, assigning a procurator and *fiskal* to each College. Even so corruption proved a seemingly ineradicable evil. Not only was it firmly rooted in Muscovite practice, but it was an inevitable consequence of the low salaries which lack of funds made necessary. Corruption was the lubricant which kept the creaking machinery of government in motion. Peculation was rife among Peter's closest associates, Menshikov being the worst, but by no means the only offender. The *Ober-fiskal* himself, the chief inspector of state, was arraigned for embezzlement and executed in 1724. Yaguzhinsky told Peter to his face that all his officials took bribes.

The Provinces

Local government was a comparative failure, despite successive attempts at reorganization. In the 1700s, the most urgent task was simply to keep order, to quell the revolts which erupted across the country and impeded the war effort. Peter's answer was to divide Russia into eight military regions or *gubernii*, each ruled by a military governor with extensive powers of policing and repression. Each *guberniya* was responsible for billetting and provisioning the regiments stationed within its bounds (1709).

Ten years later, Peter tried to lay down a more permanent settlement, this time on the basis of the Swedish model. He increased the number of *gubernii* to eleven, and divided them into *provintsii*, the main administrative units. There were fifty *provintsii* in all, each of which was further subdivided into districts. The *provintsiya* was ruled by a military governor or *voevoda*, assisted by a large and impressive staff of officials. While the *voevoda*'s main tasks were military and fiscal, he was also authorized to satisfy social needs: to build roads, schools, hospitals and orphanages, and to ensure the peasants' protection from abuse. Most of the welfare-schemes, however, existed only on paper. The *voevoda*, under constant pressure from St Petersburg for money and recruits, had little time for civilian needs. The most important members of his staff were those whose functions corresponded with the most pressing needs of the state: the *val'dmeister*, who commandeered timber for the navy: the *proviant-meister*, who requisitioned supplies for the commissariat; and the *kamerir*, who supervised the collection of taxes. At all times, the *voevoda*'s first duty—which he ignored at his peril—was to see that they carried out these tasks.

Peter's attitude to the provincial officials was contradictory: he expected them both to show initiative and to follow precise instructions. For if they veered by a hair's breadth from written regulations, they were liable to be investigated by the *fiskals* and impeached by the Procurator-General. Most officials chose to keep on the safe side of the law, and refused to take even the most obvious decisions without written orders from above, acting, as Peter complained, like a servant, who, 'seeing his master drowning, would not save him until he had satisfied himself whether it was laid down in his contract that he should pull him out of the water'. The main concern of the officials, as Menshikov reported, was to keep favour with the authorities at St Petersburg by squeezing taxes out of the locals.

Besides, attention to civilian needs was made difficult by Peter's rigorous economies. While borrowing his complex administrative apparatus from Sweden, Peter spent less on it than the Swedes had spent on the one province of Livonia. Not only were funds commonly unavailable for the founding of schools and hospitals; frequently there was not even sufficient to cover government salaries. In 1720, the *voevoda* of Archangel complained that he and his staff had not been paid for three years running. By 1725, salaries were being cut, delayed, paid in kind, or not paid at all. Inevitably, the officials resorted to time-honoured practice, and recouped their losses at the expense of the luckless civilians. Bribery and extortion were as rife in the provinces as at St Petersburg. Indeed, in 1726, immediately after Peter's death, the government decreed that only the highest officials could be paid their salaries; the rest were formally authorized to accept gratuities!

Within a few years of its inception the new system was a crumbling façade. Administration passed into the hands of the army, in the shape of local garrisons stationed in the provinces after the war. The country was redivided yet again, this time into regimental districts, which cut across or overlapped the existing provinces. In theory the army was supposed to co-operate with the civilian authorities; in fact it replaced them. At first, only regimental commanders had the right to override decisions of the *voevoda*; but soon, not only officers, but sergeants, corporals and even private soldiers were intervening directly in administration and calling the highest officials to account. In 1723, the *voevoda* of Tver' and his entire staff were gaoled for delays in tax-collection—at the order of a private soldier. The same fate overtook the vice-president of Moscow *guberniya*. By 1725, it was the army which gathered provisions and taxes, rounded up recruits and runaway serfs, policed the countryside and meted out its own military justice. Clearly, no civilian government could survive such inroads on its authority.

Attempts to stimulate municipal self-government also fell flat. In 1721, Peter ordered all towns to reorganize their affairs after the manner of the newly-acquired Baltic cities of Riga and Reval. Wealthy merchants were to elect from among their number a town council, which, under the supervision of a Chief Magistracy at St Petersburg, should run its own affairs independently. This was a particularly heavy-handed example of westernization. In the first place, apart from St Petersburg and Moscow, Russian towns were hardly more than over-grown villages, with mixed and shifting populations. The merchants were not the equivalent of western burghers and took little interest in civic matters, which they saw as a distraction from trade. Their reluct-ance was not unreasonable since any deficits in the municipal budget had to be paid for out of the councillors' own pockets. In any case, the town councils were politically hamstrung, being at the beck and call of higher authorities—the Chief Magistracy, or, more often, the local garrisons. In short, the town councillors were simply another arm of the central government, employed to collect taxes and recruits from the townsfolk. As with civilian welfare in the provinces, municipal auto-nomy was a piece of wishful thinking on Peter's part. Both were scrapped within a few years of his death.

Law and Order

Peter accepted the desirability of judicial reform as an essential part of a 'regulated' state and a precondition of general stability and economic prosperity. But the more pressing problems of war, finance, industry and administration left him little time to attend to it. At first, he attempted to break with custom by separating justice and administra-tion; but the break was short-lived. Not only was the idea too novel to grasp, but there was such a dearth of trained lawyers that bureaucrats were necessarily taking over judicial functions. There were ten judicial court circuits by 1725, each with its own assize-court. Procedure was slow and laborious, based on a code of laws last revised in 1649. Typically, Peter tried to speed up legal procedure by decreeing that accused persons might be tried in absentia, 'in order to avoid wasting time'. He tried several times to have the laws updated, but the only code in which the rights and duties of the subject were clearly delineated was the *Military Statute* of 1716. On its promulgation, therefore, Peter declared that its criminal law section should also be applied in the civil courts. The draconian articles of war, intended as a deterrent to military insubordination, were thus extended to the entire population, with dire results. The death penalty became mandatory for over a hundred offences. Lesser penalties included physical mutilation (brand-ing, and slashing of the tongue and nostrils) and hard labour in Siberia or the galley-fleet. Sentences invariably included specified degrees of knouting.

Among the earliest, most lasting and most sinister of Peter's institutions was the Secret Chancery, or *Preobrazhensky Prikaz*, the organ for the rooting out of political opposition. The *Preobrazhensky Prikaz* was a state within the state. Under its dreaded chief, Romodanovsky, its powers were supreme and all-embracing, extending to all institutions and classes. Any expression of protest or discontent with the regime was now classed as a treasonable offence; and intent to commit an offence was regarded as equivalent to its commission. A vast range of acts and statements, hitherto purely private concerns, now became police-matters, and were referred directly to the *Preobrazhensky Prikaz*. The Chancery operated through a sordid system of public informers. Neighbour was encouraged to spy on neighbour by the prospect of receiving the goods of the convicted party as his reward. To secure its convictions, the Chancery relied on confessions exacted under torture, this being the regular and statutory means of establishing evidence. If the accused denied his guilt, he was hoisted from a strappado and subjected to between one and three degrees of torture. If he maintained his innocence throughout, he was acquitted, and his accuser was put to the same test.

The vast majority of those who fell into the Chancery's clutches were ordinary peasants or townsfolk who happened to let slip some unguarded remark construed as hostile to the authorities. They included many Old Believers, who openly identified Peter with the long-predicted Antichrist. But the Chancery was no respecter of persons, and not even the highest in the land were above suspicion. Peter was ruthless in his determination to stamp out opposition. In 1699, when the *Strel'tsy* took advantage of his absence in the west to mutiny, he hastened home to have the entire corps arrested, tried and publicly beheaded. Wherever rebellion broke out among the national minorities, he smashed it without mercy.

The hopes of many Russians, churchmen, members of the old nobility and common folk alike, centred on the Czarevich Alexei, Peter's son by his first wife. Pious, bookish and indolent, Alexei was continually at odds with his domineering father, who feared a reversal of his policies under a weak successor, and tried to bully him into a change of heart. In 1716, Alexei fled to Vienna, where his brother-in-law, the Emperor Charles VI, granted him asylum within the Habsburg dominions. Peter spared no effort to secure his extradition, even threatening armed intervention, and sent special emissaries to cajole and browbeat him into submission. Eventually, Alexei agreed to return to Russia on condition that his life was spared. On his arrival, however, Peter forced him to renounce his right of succession to the throne, and instructed the Secret Chancery to organize a series of inquisitions and show-trials with the object of exposing his son's associates and making an example of them. Among those incriminated were respected churchmen and nobles, whose only offence lay in their disapproval of Peter and his methods. Peter had them publicly executed with every refinement of torture. Despite his father's pledge, Alexei himself was convicted of treasonable conspiracy and died after torture. The evidence against him was of the flimsiest, and Peter's motives in eliminating him were plainly political: to ensure the continuity of his policies and to demonstrate the penalties for slackening or hankering after old ways.

The Church

Peter reckoned himself a good Christian, knew his Bible, and sang lustily during divine service. But his religious views smacked more of Lutheranism than of Orthodoxy. Though he, no less than the Church, saw the hand of God in all things, he had no time for passive resignation, mysticism, elaborate ritual or contemplative devotion. To him, salvation demanded active and earnest endeavour, the selfless performance of practical duties, good citizenship and hearty zeal in the service of the state. He bitterly resented the Church's blind bigotry and parrot-like condemnation of all things new and foreign. He himself was frequently the object of Patriarchal sermons against such habits as shaving the beard and smoking, impious in the eyes of the Church. He retaliated by holding blasphemous parodies of Church ceremonial in the course of drunken revels with his cronies. On the political level, he resolved to have done with the Church's anti-western prejudice, and to put an end to its divisive claims on the loyalties of his subjects.

On the Patriarch's death in 1700, Peter forbade the appointment of a successor. For the present, the office was to lie vacant. Then, in 1721, it was abolished outright. Church affairs were transferred to a board of hand-picked bishops, each sworn to Peter's allegiance, and presided over by a lay-official, the *Oberprokuror*. This board, the so-called Spiritual College or Holy Synod, was in fact simply another department of state, a ministry of religious affairs, as dependent on the state as any other College. The clergy were now merely state functionaries, salaried officials, and poorly salaried at that. Significantly, all decisions of the Holy Synod were stamped: 'By order of His Imperial Majesty'; and when some daring churchman ventured to express the hope that a Patriarch might some day be reappointed, Peter pointedly retorted: 'I am your Patriarch!' The Church was turned into an important instrument for the promotion of education, and more particularly for the dissemination of state propaganda.

The Church was the greatest single landowner in Russia. Now its funds lay at the disposal of the state. Desperate for money, Peter did not hesitate to divert ecclesiastical revenues into the state coffers whenever the need arose.

Peter had no time for monasticism, regarding monks and nuns as 'parasites', and holy orders as an escape from social duties. He discouraged young people from taking vows; closed down smaller monasteries; forbade the building of new ones; and demanded that the rest should be turned over to practical good works as hospitals, orphanages, and almshouses for his veterans.

Peter's attitude toward the Old Believers and other dissenting sects was a mixture of tolerence and self-interest. While granting them freedom of worship, he insisted that they pay twice as much tax as the Orthodox and 'in this way prove of use to the state'.

Peter had an enthusiastic spokesman in Feofan Prokopovich. Formerly rector of the theological academy at Kiev, Prokopovich was raised by Peter to archbishop of Novgorod, vice-president of the Synod and virtual primate of Russia. A scholar of wide humanistic learning, who had studied under the Jesuits in Poland and Italy, he was a fervent advocate of rationalism and secular knowledge, and believed that the church should serve as the faithful handmaiden of the state in the advancement of social progress. In his numerous and oft-published sermons, he hailed Peter's achievements with fulsome rapture and claimed for them divine sanction. Victories by land and sea, the opening of factories, the spread of education and science, the suppression of opposition, all received his indiscriminate blessing. He justified the subordination of church to state, berated the lethargy and ignorance of the clergy, and in the *Spiritual Regulation* which he drew up for the Church in 1721, urged improvements in learning and discipline. The clergy should be the mouthpiece of absolution, stressing the necessity of unconditional submission to authority. 'Preachers,' he declared, 'are to preach zealously concerning the dignity and authority of those in office, especially the most high power of the czar'. They were also to recite government decrees from the pulpit and ensure universal attendance at church so that the decrees should be heard.

Though the formal separation of church and state in 1667 had foreshadowed further secularization, Peter's total amalgamation of the Church within the state had profound and far-reaching consequences. The Muscovite Church, though rooted in bigotry and superstition, could yet claim to be a bastion of conscience and morality. Its appeal to the spiritual sphere could transcend the world of politics. Under Peter, its role was transformed. It became simply the agency through which the state extended its control over the minds of its subjects. Not even the secrets of the confessional remained inviolate, but where state security might be concerned, were to be passed on to the Secret Chancery. The Church under Peter and Prokopovich taught that the whole duty of man was to serve Caesar, and that there was no salvation outside the state.

3

A Nation in Harness

Industry and the War-Effort

Defeat at Narva taught Peter the need for a determined and thorough-going exploitation of Russia's resources, with a view to the strengthening and maintenance of her armed forces. Realizing that economic self-sufficiency was the precondition of military power and political grandeur, Peter placed rapid technological advance in the forefront of his policies. It was, indeed, one of the most important achievements of the reign, being no less vital to Russia's emergence as a Great Power than success in war. In a very real sense it may be said that the victories of Poltava and Hango were won in the Ural foundries and the St Petersburg shipyards. Technological advance also made Russia very largely self-supporting in war materials, and even able to produce a surplus. Acting on the principles of contemporary mercantilism, Peter aimed not only at bringing Russia to an economic level with the west, but also at making her economically independent, capable of thriving by her own resources and efforts.

Agriculture, however, remained in a primitive condition despite Peter's efforts to encourage new methods. He had little impact on a peasantry whose way of life had hardly changed since the Middle Ages. In areas close to the front, farming was seriously disrupted by the mass drafting of peasants into the army. But even in the traditional farming region of central Muscovy, peasants still followed the wasteful age-old practice of cultivating forest-clearings for thirty years or so, and having exhausted them, moving on to fresh clearings. Despite Peter's introduction of the light wooden plough with iron ploughshare, use of the old medieval hook-plough was still widespread. Across the country, the three-field system prevailed. Little effort was made to fertilize the over-worked land, or let it lie fallow. Everywhere harvests were low,

1 Bronze bust of Peter the Great by Rastrelli the
Elder, 1724
(*The Hermitage, Leningrad*)

II The Twelve Colleges, St. Petersburg. Oil painting by an unknown artist of the second half of the eighteenth century from a drawing by M. Makhaev.

(Russian State Museum, Leningrad)

III Forge.   Engraving by G. Henning, 1735.

compared to western Europe—as a rule, they were barely above subsistence-level. The disadvantages of primitive methods were compounded by natural disasters. Famine struck the whole country between 1704 and 1706; and in the terrible years 1722 and 1723 whole villages kept alive on a diet of acorns mixed with linseed.

But though the peasants might starve, the government took care that the armed forces were well supplied with food and other necessities. To meet the needs of the shipyards, the forests were made the preserve of the Admiralty. The woods around St Petersburg were placed out of bounds, and persons felling the trees for their own use faced the death penalty.

The army's most urgent need was to replace the artillery and ammunition lost at Narva. The existing works at Tula were enlarged; but Russia's most productive ironworks were newly founded in the Urals. Here, an abundance of ore, timber and water-power, all in ideal proximity, led to a massive output of pig-iron. Because of the thousand-mile distance from the Urals to the front, a second industrial region was developed at St Petersburg and in Karelia. Both regions produced a steady flow of heavy guns and ammunition. Small arms were manufactured at Tula, which by 1711 was putting out a yearly 40,000 muskets, and later at Sestroretsk near St Petersburg. Gunpowder was produced in the Ukraine.

The second military requirement was cloth. Factories were set up to supply canvas and rope for the navy, and to process jute, linen and wool for uniforms. Peter hoped that the army's needs could be met by a domestic cloth industry; and although his forces still relied on British imports, a significant number of cloth-mills were established, in the region of Moscow, supplemented by dye and chemical works. Other new enterprises included cement-works, for the building of towns, fortresses and canals; and paper-mills, to meet the demands of the new bureaucracy. Though the needs of the private consumer came low on his list of priorities, Peter also encouraged the setting-up of a small number of workshops specializing in the manufacture of carriages, furniture, tapestries and other appurtenances of gracious living which he wished to see installed at his new capital.

Industrialization was carried out on a grand scale and with remarkable speed. While only fifteen industrial enterprises existed in Russia at the turn of the century, by 1725 there were over 200. The metallurgical and textile industries came first, with forty ironworks and some thirty cloth-mills, followed by timber-mills, paper-mills, and leatherworks. At Peter's instigation, some of the latest mechanical devices were adopted. Blast-furnaces and cotton-mills were powered by water-mills, and even spinning-jennies and mechanical saws were introduced. The basic means of production, however, in Russia as in the west, remained manual labour; and since there were few skilled native craftsmen, Russian light industry tended to be lacking in quality. Dependence on foreign experts and foremen was fairly high: five per cent of all workers at Moscow and thirteen per cent at St Petersburg, were foreigners.

How was industry financed and directed? The main impetus came from the state itself, especially in the early years of the war. The state demanded industrial development to meet its military needs. It was the largest single consumer and disposed of the biggest reserves of capital; it therefore fostered industrialization through direct investment and supervision. The Colleges of Mines and Manufactures built ironworks, shipyards and cloth-mills, staffed them with state functionaries, usually army officers, and provided labour through forced peasant levies.

Peter also tried to reproduce in Russia the energy and initiative of the western burghers, pushing his merchants into industry by alternate threats and incentives. From 1712, merchants were required to invest a percentage of their trade-profits in industry; later, state-enterprises were thrust directly into their hands. Although as a class they tended to avoid the entrepreneurial role being foisted upon them, there were exceptions, such as the Demidov family, who took over a large number of iron-works in the Urals and amassed a vast private fortune. Peter also pushed the nobles into industry, particularly his own aides and ministers. Menshikov and Shafirov both bought up cloth-mills and silkworks. By 1725, over half the factories had been transferred into private hands. The real driving force, however, was still the state, which furnished subsidies, credit facilities, tax incentives and high preferential tariffs, as well as cheap labour.

With industrial growth, the problem of internal communications became acute. Russian roads, usually earthen tracks topped with planks, were notoriously inadequate, especially in the rainy season, causing long delays and high costs. The journey from St Petersburg to Moscow alone could take five weeks. Abandoning plans for the con-struction of stone highways as too costly, Peter began work on a net-work of canals, designed to make use of the existing river system and to join the industrial hinterland with the military front and the Baltic. A canal linking St Petersburg with the Volga was opened in 1708, though it had to be closed for repairs immediately after, while a system of locks and sluices was installed. In 1718, work began on a canal to join the Neva and the Volkhov, skirting the stormy Lake Ladoga. This was completed in 1732. More successful was the joining-up of the Urals with the Baltic. Barge-loads of pig-iron, cannons and shells were carried by river from the Urals to the Volga, and thence by canal to St Petersburg for delivery to the front or shipment abroad.

As the war gradually turned in Russia's favour, Peter was able to give more attention to his second economic aim; the promotion of overseas trade. From Poltava onwards, the economy was well able to keep pace with war needs; and by 1716, with victory clearly in sight, there was leisure for long-term planning. A fresh crop of ironworks sprang up in the Urals, and the arsenal at Sestroretsk was turned over to the export-drive. By 1725, Russia was, after Sweden and England, Europe's third greatest iron-exporter. Her other exports included traditional Muscovite wares, timber, leather, tallow and furs, and now, from the Baltic provinces, flax, hemp, sailcloth, and cordage. Despite Peter's tense diplomatic relations with George I, the British admiralty was always a ready buyer of naval supplies. By 1725, Russia enjoyed a highly favourable trade balance, with exports exceeding imports by one hundred per cent. Imports consisted mainly of luxury goods for the nobility: wines, coffee, sugar, and silks; and dyes and woollens for the manufacture of uniforms.

Trade with the west expanded with the founding of St Petersburg in 1703. The city was intended not only as Russia's administrative capital, but also as the emporium of her trade and commerce. Within six months of its foundation, a Dutch merchantman, the first foreign vessel to put in at the new capital, dropped anchor in the Neva. Peter gave orders for her master and crew to be amply rewarded as an encouragement to other traders. By 1714, 16 foreign ships were docking annually at St Petersburg; and ten years later—180.

Peter failed to create a merchant marine: as in Muscovite times, Russian trade was snapped up by foreign skippers, mainly Dutch and English. For many years, too, there was rivalry between St Petersburg and Archangel. Merchants were loathe to quit the older port and hazard their goods on the Baltic, where they might fall prey to Swedish privateers. Peter had to compel them to patronize St Petersburg by decreeing that one-third of Russia's exports must pass through it and in 1724, he levied a 25 per cent tariff on goods entering or leaving Archangel. These measures had their effect: by 1725, Archangel had declined in favour of her Baltic rivals. The importance of Riga, Narva and Vyborg was transformed: from peripheral outposts of the Hanseatic League, they now lay at the heart of Russia's growing commerce.

Society in Harness

Duties and privileges in the new Russia were allocated according to a strict principle of usefulness to the state. This applied to Russians and non-Russians alike. In the Baltic provinces, the resident German landowning nobility and the city merchants, more westernized than their Russian counterparts, were allowed to retain their provincial and municipal autonomy. The Baltic nobles, who simply switched their allegiance from Sweden to Russia, were later to play a dominating, even domineering part in the government of the Empire.

A different policy operated in the Ukraine, where, after Mazepa's defection in 1708, all traces of separatism were stamped out. The Ukraine's political and economic assimilation within the empire was accelerated; Ukrainian lands were distributed to Russian nobles; a Russian resident ruled at Kiev, backed by two regiments. After 1722 the traditional office of hetman fell into enforced abeyance, the Ukraine being ruled as a province direct from St Petersburg.

Measures sterner still were applied to Russia's more backward people, the Finnish and Tartar tribes of the Middle Volga and the Bashkirs of the Urals. Despised as heathens and aliens, they were driven from their ancestral lands in hundreds of thousands by advancing Russian colonists and prospectors, and pressed into slavery in the new mines and factories.

Scarcely less severe in principle and often in practice too was Peter's attitude to the Russians themselves, all of whom became liable for service in one form or another.

All classes were subject to a bewildering diversity of indirect taxes, some forty in all. These were levied not only on luxuries, such as tobacco, melons and chess-sets, but also on daily commodities, such as salt, cucumbers and coffins; on the use of mills, fishing-streams and baths, and even on the wearing of beards.

Peter hoped to turn his merchants into the sort of thriving burghers he had seen in England and Holland by furnishing them with factory-premises, subsidies and cheap labour, and by offers of municipal and judicial autonomy. But his favours were ill-received. The merchants, a tiny class in any case, were traditionally among the most conservative of his subjects, with neither the skills nor the inclination to assume the role thrust upon them. They were mostly small-town traders, who wished to be left alone and resented municipal self-government as an arduous and time-wasting imposition. They insisted on retaining their traditional dress and beards and the more successful among them were often Old Believers, hostile to the secular state, and conducting business with their fellow-dissenters.

Nobility and Service

As in Muscovy, the role of the nobility under Peter was that of a ruling elite; but it was an elite substantially broadened and modernized. The tasks of government were new, complex and innumerable: the number of civilian posts alone almost doubled. To man these posts successfully required new attitudes and skills, which the Muscovite nobility was not always predisposed to learn. In the seventeenth century, its outlook had been blinkered and its efficiency impaired by a concept of precedence which placed a premium on the ancestral service-record of a family regardless of its current qualifications. The effect of this system, which was abolished only in 1682, still lingered. To force the old nobility to adapt itself more quickly to his requirements, Peter insisted that henceforth noble status should depend on individual merit; and conversely that state-service was now the full-time profession of the noble and a corollary of noble status. Though this shift of emphasis from blue blood to service had its roots in Muscovy, under Peter it reached its apogee. The Table of Ranks (1722) stamped the nobility with the indelible hallmark of service.

Under the Table of Ranks, positions in the armed forces and civil service were divided into fourteen parallel grades, or ranks. All comers were eligible to serve, and on starting their career at the bottom rank, received patents of personal nobility for life. On reaching the eighth rank from the top, they were awarded hereditary nobility. For outstanding candidates, Peter introduced the new titles of baron and count. Many talented outsiders—foreigners and even commoners, succeeded in working their way up the Table of Ranks, to the annoyance of the

Muscovite nobility. Yaguzhinsky, a Lithuanian, and Shafirov, a Jew, were two well-known examples. But the most spectacular rise from rags to riches was that of Menshikov, Peter's bosom-friend and hench-man. Menshikov, who reputedly began by hawking pies in the streets of Moscow, quickly rose to become commander-in-chief of the army, governor-general of St Petersburg and one of the wealthiest landowners of the day. He received from Peter, as a supreme accolade, the title of Prince, normally a prerogative of the blue-blooded, and, indeed, the only such award until the reign of Paul. Next to Peter himself, Menshi-kov and Yaguzhinsky were probably the most powerful men in Russia.

Yet the old nobility, much as they complained of plebeian upstarts, were not in fact displaced by an influx of commoners, as is often sup-posed. The top military and civil ranks—the *Generalitet*, as it was called —continued in the main to be staffed by members of the old nobility, Sheremetev, for example, in the army, and Romodanovsky in the Secret Chancery. Furthermore, families with a pedigree of over a hundred years automatically retained their hereditary nobility, regard-less of service. On the other hand, power and prestige now lay with rank, not with birth; and though titles of nobility were hereditary, official rank was not, but had to be earned through service. Nobility brought few advantages of itself. It was cheapened through equal inheritance by all the sons in a family, which created a proliferation of titled nobodies, each with a meagre slice of the family fortune. So numerous was the princely house of Golitsyn, for example, that it was commonly asked whether such-and-such a Golitsyn was 'one of the rich ones or the poor ones?'

State-service was a lifelong compulsory obligation, which allowed of little, if any, leisure. Retirement was permitted only in cases of terminal illness or hopeless debility. Compassionate leave was seldom granted, still less leave between campaigns or assignments. Petitioning the Senate for compassionate leave in 1727, a brigadier complained that he had not set eyes on his estates since 1700. Penalties for evasion of service included exile, physical mutilation and 'civil death', a deprivation of all rights, leaving the culprit an 'unperson' in the eyes of the law, and signal proof of the complete identification of nobility with service.

Before commencing service proper, the young noble underwent five years of compulsory grounding in arithmetic and geometry, followed by a state examination. The successful candidates started out on the

Table of Ranks; those who failed were automatically drafted into the navy, the least popular branch of the service, and were formally forbidden to marry! Two-thirds of all candidates were channelled into the armed forces. They began by attending one of the new military academies (Naval, Engineering and Artillery), or by undergoing specialist training abroad. After this, they received a commission, usually in one of the newly formed imperial Guards regiments (Semyonovsky, Preobrazhensky and Horse Guards) from where in turn they would be sent out to command other units across the country.

There was considerable mobility between the military and bureaucratic branches of the service, and a noble was commonly required to hold a succession of different posts in the course of his career. But the prestige of the army was markedly higher than that of the bureaucracy, and the military style of life was dominant and all-pervasive. The army officer, transferred to a civilian post, brought with him the same insistence on form and discipline which had been drilled into him in the army. This tended to lend the bureaucracy its peculiarly rigid, mechanical and impersonal stamp. Orders from St Petersburg were carried out without question, regardless of local interests or desires, the personal feelings of the official concerned, or even common sense. The way to promotion was through prompt obedience and working by the rules laid down in the *General Regulation*; individual initiative was frowned on. Moreover the state, in the persons of the *Ober-fiskal* and Procurator-General, kept careful watch on all officials to ensure that orders were obeyed. Confiscation of property and imprisonment were among the lesser penalties prescribed for disobedience. Thus the bureaucracy tended to become a state-oriented, inward-looking caste, isolated from the people it governed.

State service had other effects on the nobleman's outlook, which served to differentiate him still further from his western counterpart. By permanently removing him from his birthplace and estates, the state cut him off from territorial allegiances. Obliged to make the service his career, he came to forget that he was a landowner from a particular locality, and knew only that he was an officer in the imperial service. His loyalties were to the army, the regiment and the state. Even the Prussian Junker, comparable in many ways to the Russian noble, still retained his local attachments. But the Russian felt no special ties of sentiment to any province or district. His estates he left for relatives or hired bailiffs to run. His lands and serfs he bought and sold according to the profit-motive, whether in Russia or in newly conquered lands, such as the Ukraine and Bashkiria. He showed little of that local patriotism or corporate pride which in the west could pose a real threat to absolutist authority.

In return for state-service, the noble was accorded certain privileges. He was exempted from direct taxation and confirmed in his exclusive right to own lands and serfs. Furthermore, by his Entail Law of 1714, Peter decreed the indivisibility of landed estates. These 'privileges', however, are rather to be understood as further aspects of state-service. Land-ownership was bound up with responsibility for recruiting, tax-collection and policing on the estate, the noble acting as the agent of the central government. As for the Entail Law, Peter's aim was not so much to enhance the standing of the noble families, as to bolster the tax-yielding capacity of their estates by prohibiting their subdivision among numerous heirs; and in addition, to create a reserve of landless younger sons, whom economic necessity as well as legal compulsion, should induce into the service. In any case, the Entail Law ran full tilt against patriarchal Muscovite practice. Unlike their British counter-parts, the Russian nobles regarded inheritance by a single heir as un-godly and unjust, and secured the repeal of the Law after Peter's death.

Serfdom

Though no class escaped the burdens imposed by the struggle for Great Power status, by far the heaviest lot fell to the peasantry. It was they who fought in the rank and file of the army, rowed the galleys, built the factories, ports and canals, and toiled in shipyard, mine and factory. The state coffers were replenished chiefly at their expense. Muscovite history had seen the gradual enserfment of a once-free peasantry. The state, needing a fixed source of taxes and services, gradually tied the peasant to the land. Peter, with his incomparably greater and more urgent needs, was responsible for a marked intensifi-cation of this process. Abolishing various surviving categories of free or semi-free peasant, he assigned all peasants to two main classes, roughly equal in number: the bonded serfs, belonging to the nobility; and the 'state peasants', or serfs living on crown lands and now placed at the disposal of the state, for employment in building and industrial projects.

The army required a constant intake of peasant recruits, to make good its losses and raise its fighting potential. In the first dozen years of the century, it absorbed an annual quota of 22,000 men. At first, only bachelors were liable to conscription; but after 1708, it was extended to married men and fathers. The upper age-limit rose from twenty to forty; and for the Pruth campaign, men of fifty were called up. Service was for twenty-five years; in practice this usually meant for life. Once drafted, a conscript was unlikely to see his home or family again. Casualties were heavy: those in the first decade of the century, through battle, disease or desertion, are put at 100,000; and mortality in the Russian navy was reckoned to be double that of any other. Desertion presented the authorities with a chronic problem. Peter strove to check it through the ferocious penalties of his Military Statute. Notorious was the '*shpitsrut*', or running the gauntlet.

State serfs were forcibly uprooted from their villages and sent to work wherever the need arose: to build ships, fortresses and towns, to lay roads and dig mines and canals. Forty thousand were rounded up annually for the construction of St Petersburg, where they sickened and died in their thousands amid the fever-ridden swamps of the Neva. Others were transported to the Urals to toil in the mines and factories. In contrast to the privileged and well-paid foreign artisans, these Russian workers were hardly more than slave-labourers. They were paid just enough to keep them from starvation, the money used for this being recouped from their home villages. At work, they were fenced in like prisoners and guarded by sentries to prevent escapes. To boost his labour-force, Peter scoured the country for fresh conscripts, rounding up prisoners-of-war, deserters, vagrants and criminals.

The bonded serfs were the unpaid labourers and legal chattels of the noble on whose land they lived and which they were now forbidden to leave without his authorization. In return for small allotments which he permitted them to cultivate for their own needs, the serfs were shackled with permanent statutory obligations towards him. These were of two main kinds. In the central and southern provinces, they performed labour on his lands, usually two or three days a week—the *corvée* system. In the infertile north, they paid a yearly quitrent in cash, kind or both. The noble was invested with sweeping rights over his serfs. He determined the amount of *corvée* or quitrent. He was responsible for tax-collecting and selecting recruits for the army. He took charge of keeping order on his estates and meted out his own rough justice.

In his momentous decision to tie the peasant to the noble rather than to the land, Peter's main intention was to compensate the noble for his services to the state. In a mainly rural economy, desperately short of capital, it was an obvious expedient to pay the noble in terms of serfs (or 'souls' as the male peasants, with unconscious irony, were officially termed). Serfs came readier to hand than silver. While he hoped that the nobles would not abuse their authority, Peter took few steps to check them. In his view, all must work for the state according to their condition, the serf for the noble, the noble for the czar. Times were hard, and each must do his duty without complaint. If the serf was genuinely oppressed by his master, said Peter, it was always open to him to volunteer for army-service.[7]

The burden of taxation (which all but tripled with spiralling war-costs), fell almost wholly on the peasants. Muscovite revenue derived mainly from indirect taxes, a source which Peter continued to exploit fully. But his expenses were so great that he relied far more on the capitation tax, which indeed became his largest single source of revenue. The traditional tax-unit was the peasant household; but a census in 1710 revealed a marked decrease in the number of households as peasants crowded under the same roof to ease the financial burden. After a new census in 1719, the tax unit was transferred to the individual, and an annual uniform poll-tax was levied on all 'souls', including old men, invalids and children. No account was taken of an individual's capacity to pay, the size and yield of the land he worked, or the number of his dependents (or whether they had moved away or died since the last census). Thus a poor peasant with three children paid twice as much tax as a richer peasant with one child. It is reckoned that the average tax burden of a peasant in the 1710s equalled almost two-thirds of the market value of the grain which he harvested from his allotment: a fearfully heavy imposition. Peter's only concern, however, was to balance his budget; if the peasant was ruined in the process, that was a regrettable necessity.

The exactions of the civil authorities, the *kamerir* and *voevoda*, were bad enough; but when the army stepped in to take over provincial rule in 1723, the suffering was beyond endurance. Three times a year, a military *komissar* and his troops made their grim progress from village to village. 1723 was the second successive year of appalling famine. The military were inexorable. Peasants with cattle or personal belongings had to sell them to pay the tax. For those without belongings the only solution was flight; and in these last terrible years of Peter's reign, thousands of peasants fled their homesteads, singly or with their families. Sometimes whole communities vanished overnight. In Kazan *guberniya*, over half the peasants were reported missing; and in Russia as a whole between 1719 and 1727 there were 200,000 recorded fugitives. The army followed on their heel, bringing cruel retaliation. Special punitive decrees were issued. Anyone who harboured a fugitive would have his lands confiscated; if a priest, he would be unfrocked. A peasant who informed on his fellow would receive his freedom. The military behaved, said Menshikov, 'not like shepherds, but like wolves'.

4

Education and 'Westernization'

Peter's view of education was practical and utilitarian: knowledge to him was the key to power. But by knowledge he meant the secular, technological and scientific knowledge of the west, not the great body of Orthodox doctrine and learning handed down by the Church. On the contrary, Peter sought to destroy the Church's monopoly in the field of thought and ideas. Russia's need was not for more 'longbeards' (as he slightingly dubbed his clergy) with their metaphysical cosmology, their sterile scholasticism and their indiscriminate condemnation of the west—but for experts in every field of technology. Recruitment of foreigners was only an interim measure: Russia must produce her own technicians: shipwrights and navigators, draftsmen and engineers, gunsmiths and artillerists, diplomats and jurists. For these purposes the existing educational institutions, the theological academies of Moscow and Kiev, were clearly inadequate.

Peter's first resource, especially earlier in his reign, was to send groups of young nobles abroad at state expense, to England, Holland, France, Italy and elsewhere, to pick up at random whatever skills they might: languages, for example, or seamanship, or mechanics. This was a haphazard experiment: often the young men dallied in ale-houses and brothels, and returned with only a smattering of knowledge . Even so, their contact with the outside world had its uses: it helped stimulate a general thirst for knowledge of the west among the young, in contrast to their more staid and hidebound elders. More valuable experience, however, was probably gained at the official level, during the occupation of northern Germany and in the course of establishing diplomatic and commercial missions abroad.

Peter also founded technical schools at home. In 1701, a School of Mathematics and Navigation was opened in Moscow by the Scots mathematician and seaman, Farquharson. In 1715, it was transferred to St Petersburg as the Naval Academy. It was soon followed by an Artillery Academy and an Engineering Academy. Other specialized training-schools were set up to provide instruction in shipbuilding, mining and medicine.

The most serious long-term need was simply for literacy and know-ledge of elementary mathematics. In 1715, graduates of the Naval Academy were sent out into the provinces to organize elementary schools or, as they were called, 'cipher-schools'. These represented Russia's first attempt at primary secular education. The experiment was too novel to take root: although there were over forty cipher-schools by 1722, only a quarter of the pupils completed the course, and most of these entered the priesthood. By 1727, only eight cipher-schools remained. Secular knowledge was still widely regarded as ungodly; mathematics was seen as a branch of sorcery, and truancy was common. Peter tried to tighten discipline and enforce attendance: one enterprising *voevoda* sent out troops to round up children from the countryside and bring them to school under escort! In the end it was the Church, which, for all its disfavour in Peter's eyes, proved the only institution capable of providing some sort of elementary education. Under the *Spiritual Regulation*, parish schools were ordered to teach mathematics, geography, history and philosophy as well as religious knowledge. In practice, however, the Church continued to teach from within an Orthodox framework, rooted in theology and scholasticism.

Towards the end of his reign, Peter tried to encourage interest in higher learning. By 1719, the capital could boast a public library and natural history museum; and shortly before his death, with the help of Leibniz and Christian Wolff, Peter laid plans for the foundation of the St Petersburg Academy of Sciences. The Academy was intended partly as a status-symbol: Peter hoped that it 'would earn us respect and honour in Europe' as a learned research-institute. But he also wanted it to be of practical benefit; and to this end, expeditions were sent out to prospect for coal and oil and explore unknown parts of the Empire. Prospectors opened up much of Siberia, and navigators charted the Baltic, Black Sea and Caspian.

While the Church continued to be an important instrument of education, several sharp blows were struck to sever its cultural and ideological grip. One such was the introduction of a secular or 'civil' alphabet, in which all non-religious publications were printed after

1710. This marked a clean symbolic break with the past: state documents, treaties, decrees and manifestoes now appeared in the new print. At Peter's order, the presses turned out scores of technical works, textbooks on navigation, astronomy, mathematics, mechanics and architecture. Among the earliest of these was a two-volume mathematical primer, *Arithmetic*, by Magnitsky, a colleague of Farquharson (1703). In 1717 appeared a translation of Huygen's *Cosmotheros*, Russia's first introduction to the Copernican system and a blow at the religious interpretation of the universe. The cumbersome slavonic numerals were replaced by the arabic system, an obvious prerequisite for mathematical, scientific and technological advance. Words and terms hitherto unheard-of flooded into the language, bringing Russians into contact with a whole new world of concepts and experiences: *algebra, logarithm, longtitude, microscope* and *anatomy* are just a few out of hundreds. Another symbol of the abandonment of the religious outlook was the adoption of the western calendar. In 1700 (7,208, by Muscovite reckoning) the Julian calendar was introduced, and the first New Year of the eighteenth century was celebrated in January, not, as hitherto, in September. New calendars were published and distributed. So were forecasts of solar and lunar eclipses, which exemplified western scientific rationalism and discredited religious superstition.

The clearest symbol of westernization was the new capital. The creation of St Petersburg, on the desolate Neva marshes, was the conscious embodiment of reasoned endeavour, intended to mark a radical break with the insular conservatism of Moscow. In contrast to Moscow's labyrinth of meandering alleys, wooden dwellings and Byzantinesque churches, St Petersburg was built in stone and designed to reflect regularity, uniformity and classical order. Along its long straight boulevards and 'prospects' palaces, public buildings and aristocratic mansions burgeoned. Parsimonious as a rule, Peter lavished money and attention on his 'paradise', as he called it, wishing to make St Petersburg and the surrounding royal townships worthy rivals of Amsterdam, Venice and Versailles.

In the first half of the reign, Peter sought to emulate the sober simplicity of seventeenth-century Holland. He gave the city the quasi-Dutch name *Pieterburkh* and had it built in a blend of Dutch, Baltic and Italianate styles, the so-called 'northern baroque'. The spirit of *Pieterburkh* is reflected in the city's first building, appropriately a military one, the Fortress of Peter and Paul, designed by the Italian-Swiss, Tressini.

Within the fortress, stern, plain and unadorned, Tressini erected the city's so-called 'cathedral', which resembles a Lutheran garrison-church in its simple unpretentiousness. After his visit to France in 1717, Peter found the grandiose baroque of Versailles more to his taste; and by the end of his reign, St Petersburg was being built to overawe with its pomp, size and decorative magnificence, as for example in the huge, sprawling administrative edifice, built (again by Tressini) to house the Colleges, or in the palladian splendour of Menshikov's palace. A host of artists and craftsmen, recruited in France and Italy, set to work embellishing the city. Typical of Peter's concern with symbolic greatness was his commission of a series of tableaux depicting the victories of the Northern War. One of the most consummate expressions of the grandeur of St Petersburg was the work of the Italian sculptor Rastrelli the Elder. Rastrelli's celebrated bronze bust of Peter, grim, determined and heroic, is the very embodiment of his strenuous, reforming absolutism.

Peter's efforts to force western social manners on his nobility were notoriously heavy-handed. Characteristic was his abolition of the beard and traditional long 'kaftan', and his enforcement of the wearing of European dress for men and women alike. Peter himself forsook the semi-sacrosanct robes of the czars of Muscovy, and usually donned military uniform. He drew up detailed statutory regulations concerning what was required of a noble by way of dress, carriage and livery, according to his rank. These measures were followed in 1718 by the Decree concerning the Assemblies, which he issued on his return from France. This decree laid down rules for the holding of regular social gatherings in private houses for the purpose of dancing, smoking and polite conversation. The Assemblies were attended by nobles, merchants and master-craftsmen, accompanied by their wives and daughters. The early Assemblies provided a ludicrous contrast to the stately model of Versailles, the Russians capering sheepishly and none too gracefully about in their unaccustomed western attire under the stern eye of the czar (himself a nimble dancer). In 1717, Peter published a translation of a German handbook on etiquette, *The Honourable Mirror of Youth*. This book, which ran to three editions in the reign, prescribed the accepted modes of salutation and address, and advised the young noble against picking his nose, belching or spitting in company, scratching his head at table, or wearing heavy boots for dancing. In particular, it underlined the different standards of behaviour expected of noble and peasant, and warned against speaking Russian in front of servants. Once their initial strangeness had worn off, these social reforms quickly caught on particularly among the young. They were especially welcome to women, now emancipated from centuries of semi-oriental seclusion.

There was little culture in the broader sense, since outside the Church there was no tradition of learning. Despite Peter's hopes, the technical books sold badly. Nor was there much enthusiasm for Russia's first newspaper, the *Moscow News* (1703), a dull and badly factual official news-sheet, giving little more than accounts of battles. The greatest demand was either for old religious favourites, especially Lives of Saints, or for translations from Ovid and Aesop and tales of western romance and chivalry. There was as yet no leisured-class to appreciate and foster *belles-lettres*, since the nobility was almost wholly preoccupied with state service. Only the wealthiest and most assured of Peter's henchmen had the means and leisure to acquire more than the outward signs of culture, and they indeed were more attracted by material opulence than by intellectual or spiritual values.

Peter's Legacy — The Leviathan-state

Historians enjoy debating how far Peter's rule was revolutionary or evolutionary. His own followers and spokesmen favoured the first interpretation: Russia, said one, had been brought 'from non-existence, as it were, into existence'. Though flattering to Peter, this was unfair to his predecessors in the seventeenth century and earlier, who had also aimed at Great Power status, though usually at a slower pace. Closer contacts with the west and the drive to the Baltic, had, after all, been keynotes of foreign policy since the thirteenth century. Moreover, Peter's dynamism, colossal as it was, did not aim at any basic change in the traditional political and social structure. Autocracy was still the essence of Russian polity. The nobility, despite realignments of its functions, remained the ruling class, its social primacy confirmed and extended. The peasant were shackled more firmly than ever to the base of the social hierarchy. Even Peter's assaults on the Church and his secularization of culture can be seen as a culmination of earlier trends.

Furthermore, 'westernization' did not mean turning Russia into a replica of Holland, Sweden, or France. On the contrary, Peter wanted Russia only to 'become herself' and realize her own potential. To do this he accelerated the application of western techniques which alone

IV The Admiralty, St. Petersburg. Engraving by A. Zubov, 1717.

Peter the Great attributed to F. Jouvenet.

VI Menshikov by Tanauer.
(*The Hermitage, Leningrad*)

VII Empress Anna attributed to L. Caravaque.   VIII Empress Elizabeth by V. Erichsen.

IX Pyotr Shuvalov by F. S. Rokotov.

could make her impregnable and self-sufficient. 'Westernization' was a means, not an end. 'We need Europe for a few decades,' Peter is reported to have said, 'then we can turn our back on her.'

Peter's role was that of a catalyst, speeding up policies already slowly under way. However, he acted with such vigour and energy that his actions certainly seemed revolutionary to those who were subjected to them. This impression was enhanced by the fact that much reform was concerned with outward appearance. The abolition of the beard and long dress was undoubted proof of revolution to those who cherished them as symbols of piety or pledges of salvation, and regarded Peter as the Antichrist for doing away with them. It was, then, the pace, volume and external aspects of reform that were revolutionary; so much so, in fact, as perhaps to constitute, after all, a real break in historical continuity. Change came so thick and fast that it marked a qualitative as well as quantitative wrench from the past; it was 'transformation' rather than 'reform'.

Peter's methods, too, were revolutionary in the eyes of the vast body of the nation, whose yearning for traditional ways was reinforced by his utter ruthlessness. How far they were justified in feeling the costs of his policies to be more than could reasonably be borne, is bound to depend on personal standpoints. Soviet historians contend that the strain, though great, was within the nation's capacity. A classic nineteenth-century historian,* on the other hand, points out that few nations, if any, have ever been called upon to make such tremendous sacrifices in such a short space of time. What is beyond dispute, however, is the loathing with which Peter's methods were held by the average subject, and the overall lack of sympathy with his aims. As one of Peter's followers complained: 'The Czar pushes uphill with a dozen supporters—millions pull downhill.' Peter was well aware of the general odium in which he and his policies were held; but this only stiffened his resolve to impose them regardless. 'Though a thing be good and necessary,' he wrote, 'yet if it be new, our people will not do it unless forced to.' He believed he was dealing with 'animals, whom I wish to turn into human-beings', and looking back in retrospect at the end of the reign, declared: 'Was it not all done by force?' In a sense, then, Peter's rule was 'revolution from above', the ruthless application of state power on the human material at its disposal.

Russia was now an absolutist state to a degree unprecedented even

* S. M. Solov'yov.

under the despotic Ivan IV. The military oath of allegiance was taken not only to the czar but also to 'the Russian state'. This new concept of the state loomed high above the nation, a huge, impersonal, meta-physical leviathan, with its own inexorable rationale. The czar was no longer simply the 'father of his people', the owner of patrimonial estates, but the 'first servant of the state', in the service of which all was per-mitted. He was answerable to no man-made laws; and with the absorption of the Church's authority by the state, there was no pressure on him even to observe the laws of God as traditionally understood. Czarevich Alexei, pointing this out, remarked of Peter: 'Human life means nothing to him; he thinks that like God he has the right of life and death.' The traditional orthodox concept of submission to the Christ-like czar was rewritten by Prokopovich in terms of western divine-right monarchy. In the *Spiritual Regulation*, and his formidable apologia of absolutism, *The True Law of the Monarch's Will*, Prokopo-vich borrowed the ideology of Grotius and Hobbes. 'The Emperor of all the Russias,' he declared, 'is an autocratic and unlimited monarch. To obey his supreme authority, not only from fear, but also from con-science, God himself commands.' As subjects of an autocrat, he argued, the Russian people had forfeited its liberty and right to criticize. The people, he declared, 'cannot judge the monarch's actions'; it must 'do everything the autocrat demands without opposition or complaint'.

Muscovite rulers had, as a rule, seen their duty in static terms of defence and internal consolidation. Peter's reforms, on the other hand, were dynamic, aimed at changing every aspect of life. The people should be brought, by force if necessary, towards certain stated ends, 'Russia's glory', 'the general welfare', 'the happiness and prosperity of the citizens'. These aims, formulated from above by the state and en-forced by police methods, bore little relation to the actual hopes and wishes of the people.

Peter's policies were not unique to Russia: the galvanization of society in the interests of military efficiency and the promotion of 'prosperity by compulsion' after all, were also characteristic of rising absolutism in the west. Russian practice could be compared with the Prussian experi-ence under Frederick-William I, from whom, indeed, Peter borrowed his harsh *Military Statute*. But certainly the speed and scale of change were more striking in Russia than elsewhere, because of the almost total absence of restraints on the state. The law gave all power to the state and no protection to the individual. No social or institutional blocks

existed to offset the naked power of the autocrat: the nobility were
agents of his will and lacked any tradition of corporate resistance; the
towns were few, small and impotent; the Church was manacled to the
state; the Senate and Colleges were in essence merely despatch-offices
where imperial orders were stamped and sealed.

Russia under Peter I broke out of the paralyzing straight-jacket of the
seventeenth century: from the Orthodox legacy of ignorance, unworld-
liness, isolationism and defeat; but these reforms bound her in the new
and far tighter shackles of the modern leviathan-state; with its foreign
commitments, its all-compassing demands and inescapable exactions;
its inroads on private life, its harsh officialdom, its rigid social divisons,
its ubiquitous *fiskals* and secret police. Peter sloughed off the spiritual
culture of Muscovy; but he took to St Petersburg the traditional
absolutism of Ivan the Terrible, the old 'amalgam of despotism and
servility'; clad it in the terminology of Grotius and Hobbes, and enforced it at bayonet-point with tens of thousands of western-style
muskets.

II

MID-CENTURY RUSSIA
1725-1762

2. Russia and the Seven Years' War.

5

The Age of 'Palace-Revolutions' 1725-1762

Peter's last years, though among the most creative of his reign, were clouded by illness and gloomy forebodings: would Russia continue after his death along the path he had set, or would she revert to older, more familiar ways, and renounce her hard-won status? The affair of the Czarevich Alexei showed how easily there might be a relapse. Determined to ensure the survival of his policies, Peter drew up a succession-law which empowered each monarch to select his own heir, and to do so regardless of birth or lineage, but on the grounds of individual merit alone (1722). Here if anywhere was the embodiment of Peter's concept of the czar as 'first servant' of the state rather than its dynastic proprietor.

But his plan for stability and continuity miscarried. By disrupting the natural and more-or-less accepted line of descent from father to son, he unwittingly helped to condemn Russia to forty years of constitutional anarchy. Between 1725 and 1762 the succession followed a wildly erratic course. A bizarre sequence of men, women and children, some not even Russian, some hardly sane (at least one neither Russian nor sane), reigned for an average of six years each. Some lasted only months, or even weeks. The majority ascended the throne not—as Peter hoped— out of considerations of fitness, but as the instruments of powerful court-factions, sometimes with the assistance of foreign agents and bribes. Each succession-crisis unleashed a new scramble for power. Each reign saw a fresh proliferation of conspiracies, cabals and counter-plots.

Crucial on each occasion was the role of the Imperial Guards. Created by Peter as a bastion of autocracy, they turned out to be a sword of Damocles to his successors. Like the Janissaries or Praetorians, the Guards were usually apolitical, and sold their services to the highest bidder. Thus, Russia's constitutional history now depended on court-intrigues and palace-revolutions. The momentum of this era extended beyond it: the notion that a group of guardsmen could decide the succession for themselves by means of a military *coup* cast its shadow across the rest of the eighteenth century and well into the nine-teenth.

The throne, it was said, was neither hereditary nor elective: it was occupative. Its incumbents lived in fear and slept fitfully, not knowing whether the morrow would see them still ensconced in the palace, or rudely deposed and under way to some remote dungeon or monastery-cell. Most of the rulers were nonentities. Real power rested with the caucuses and strong-willed favourites, who manipulated policy from behind the throne. It was they, not the nominal czars and czarinas, who ruled Russia; and their rise or fall could constitute a palace-revolution in its own right.

'Old' and 'New' Nobility 1725–1730

Peter himself delayed using his own succession-law until it was too late. In 1725, taken fatally ill with a chronic urinary complaint at the age of fifty-three, he lay speechless on his deathbed, with only strength enough to scrawl: 'Give all to —', before relapsing into a final coma. The question of the succession now degenerated into a tussle between two rival cliques. The new nobility, headed by Menshikov, were men whom Peter had raised from humble origins to fabulous power and patronage. Menshikov's influence had been second only to Peter's in the last years of the reign. Bent on retaining power, they supported the candidature of Peter's widow, dowager-empress Catherine, herself originally a common Livonian serving-maid, who had been Men-shikov's mistress before becoming Peter's. The old nobility were headed by two ancient blueblooded families, the Golitsyns and the Dolgorukys. They resented the rise of the new men, especially Menshikov, had placed their hopes in the Czarevich Alexei, and after his death trans-ferred them to his son Peter, grandson to Peter I, and his only direct descendant in the male line. The old nobility favoured a more gradual approach to westernization, and complained of the pace and strain of the late reign.

Legally, the issue should have been decided by the Senate; and indeed senators led by the old nobility had assembled for discussion at the

Winter Palace. But while they deliberated, Menshikov acted: the Guards were won over to Catherine's cause by timely payment of salary-arrears; and while the senators debated inside the palace, the Guards were drawn up outside, where, to the loud beating of drums, they declared vociferously for Catherine. Cowed by this show of force, the senators quickly succumbed.

Catherine I, middle-aged, stout and homely, chose to devote her declining years to drink, fineries and dalliance; and in 1726 delegated all authority to a Supreme Privy Council. The Council, divided among old and new nobles, was chaired by Menshikov, now factual ruler of Russia. His administrative ability was outstanding, though much of it went on feathering his own nest. In 1727, when it became clear that Catherine's days were numbered, he induced the ailing Empress to nominate her grandson Peter as successor, hoping thereby to placate the old nobility. At the same time, he pulled off a bold advantage for himself by arranging the betrothal of his daughter to the eleven-year-old heir-apparent. A few months later, on the latter's accession as Peter II, Menshikov's power reached its zenith. He augmented his already enormous private fortune, appropriated the rank of 'generalissimo', and intrigued, though unsuccessfully, to make himself Duke of Courland. But his greed and arrogance aroused general indignation. He overreached himself, and fatally neglected to ensure the continuing support of the Guards. It was now the turn of the old nobility to make a bid for power. Winning over the impressionable Peter, who was in any case ill-disposed to his domineering father-in-law, the Dolgorukys and Golitsyns had Menshikov suddenly arrested, stripped of his ranks and fortune, and, together with his daughter, banished to Siberia (1727).

The two noble families now seized power, filling the Supreme Privy Council and *Generalitet* with their own number. A young Dolgoruky, Peter's favourite, took command of the Guards, and his sister was betrothed to the Czar. All seemed set for lengthy rule by an aristocratic oligarchy. But the oligarchs' ideal of peace and retrenchment degenerated into mere license. Rejoicing in Menshikov's downfall and the prospect of a long and tranquil reign, the oligarchs abandoned St Petersburg for the old familiar capital. In Moscow, and in the surrounding hunting-lodges, as if to compensate for the privations and hardships of the past thirty years, they threw themselves into a frenzied round of hunting-parties and carousals. The court, reported the Spanish ambassador, was a 'veritable Babylon'. Few bothered to attend the meetings of the Supreme Privy Council, and day-to-day consideration of policy was virtually abandoned.

These revels came to a sudden end in the New Year of 1730, when the Czar was laid low with smallpox. On the day appointed for his wedding and coronation, he died, and the Supreme Privy Council met in sober haste to consider what action to take. The throne stood vacant. The late czar had not appointed an heir. The Council was ambitious and intelligent. It resolved not merely to decide the succession on its own authority and without outside consultation, but to make a clean break with the traditional political system and replace autocracy by limited constitutional monarchy. A similar revolution had lately taken place in Sweden, and the oligarchs were hopeful that the experiment would succeed in Russia. Their choice of candidate fell on Anna, niece to Peter I. Living in dull seclusion as widowed duchess of Courland, Anna could not normally have aspired to rule Russia in any capacity, since Peter's daughter, Elisabeth, had the prior claim. With this in mind, the oligarchs offered Anna the throne on condition she signed a formal constitution which obliged her to seek the consent of the Supreme Privy Council before taking any important decision.

As anticipated, the Duchess was happy to accept the throne on any terms, and readily agreed to rule at the Council's bidding. But her promise was soon revealed as worthless. When the Council's actions became known, there was mounting indignation. The conduct and even the authority of the Council were questioned by large numbers of nobles, old and new alike, who had flocked to Moscow for the late emperor's coronation. Once they discovered that the oligarchs were concocting a private deal, they determined to resist. The idea of imposing terms on Anna was not in itself unattractive; but the high-handedness and secrecy of the oligarchs caused deep offence. Prokopovich voiced the general discontent. Better one autocrat, said he, than multiple tyranny by the Golitsyns and Dolgorukys. As a flood of angry protests reached the empress, the oligarchs tried desperately to rally last-minute support by offering broader representation on the Council. They were forestalled, however by an abler faction of new nobles under Prokopovich, Tatishchev and Kantemir. This trio, with the backing of the Guards, arranged a public showdown in which they petitioned the empress to restore autocracy. Anna, aware that the oligarchs were outmanoeuvred, had the constitution brought to her, and claiming that she was yielding to the will of the nation, tore it up in their faces. The

Supreme Privy Council was disbanded. The Golitsyns and Dolgorukys were banished and later liquidated. The empress was crowned as autocrat. Constitutional monarchy in Russia had lasted precisely ten days.

Empress Anna and 'German' Rule 1730–1741

If the restorers of autocracy hoped that Anna would inaugurate a second era of reform, they were to be disappointed. Though she did return the seat of government to St Petersburg, the new empress mirrored the drab German backwater from which she had so unexpectedly emerged. Tall, stout and ungracious, she was a gruff, waspish harridan and though shrewd, was quite uneducated. Life in Courland had soured and narrowed her, and the manner of her accession had not improved her temper. Indolent and bored, she took little interest in government, leaving it to a so-called Cabinet of Ministers, and devoted herself to a round of tasteless frivolity, with a passion for freaks, dwarfs and buffoons. Lavish festivities raised court expenditure to three times its level under Peter I. Twice as much was spent on the imperial stables as on national education.

Anna's mistrust of the old nobility soon extended to the nobility in general. Obsessed by fears of some fresh assault on her power, she surrounded herself with a cordon of Germans, who swarmed in from Courland, Livonia and elsewhere to take over the reins of power. Ostermann ran the Cabinet. Münnich took charge of the army. Control of commerce and the iron industry passed into German hands. A fourth Guards regiment, the Izmailovsky, was formed, staffed entirely by Germans. Two dozen key positions were held by non-Russians. Foreign influences, including German, were of course nothing new, and both Ostermann and Münnich had served under Peter I. But in Peter's day, foreigners had come as technical advisers only, and were replaced whenever possible by Russian trainees. They were seldom given high executive office or admitted at court. But now, Germans were deliberately promoted above the heads of Russians, and once ensconced, seemed to have a finger in every pie. German became the language of the court, and to make the pill more bitter, members of the old Russian nobility were forced into the degrading role of court-jesters and served as the butt of Anna's malicious jokes.

Of all the Germans, the most hated was the notorious Bühren. Anna's favourite of long standing and now her High Chamberlain, he was a sinister and repulsive churl. Grasping and curmudgeonly, coarse, vindictive and unscrupulous, he used his almost unlimited influence to amass a vast private fortune and to scotch anyone who crossed his path. His haughty contempt for Russia was so brazen that his name became a by-word for alien oppression and misrule. In point of fact, he was too busy lining his pockets to spare much time for politics: he induced Anna to bestow on him the duchy of Courland, to which even Menshikov had aspired in vain. Ironically, much of the loathing which the Germans incurred arose from the zeal with which they set about checking the backsliding of the past few years. They tried to restore finances by ruthless tax accountancy and by bringing incompetent officials to book. They kept the army up to the mark by harsh discipline and drilling. They stimulated industry and tried to curb the import of foreign luxuries. But their arrogance was insupportable: and the objection was not so much that they ruled badly as that they ruled at all.

The most hateful feature of the reign was the revival of judicial terror. Anna's constant feelings of insecurity, her suspicions of the Russian nobility, and her knowledge that her German retainers were universally loathed, led to the re-emergence of the Secret Chancery and all its works. Its malicious denunciations and venal informers, arbitrary arrest and summons before the dreaded Ushakov in Moscow, the deliberate use of torture both as a means of exacting evidence and as a regular form of punishment—the entire inquisitional and punitive machinery was once more set in motion and worked at full pressure throughout the reign and in every corner of the empire. Not merely were the main offenders, the Golitsyns and Dolgorukys, singled out and eliminated; that was to be expected. The slightest breath of criticism from the meanest sections of the population was also avenged by the government with obsessive malice. For the least word, not just against the empress, but more especially against Bühren or the other German overlords, tens of thousands of ordinary people, mostly peasants, guilty of no more than a momentary indiscretion, were hauled before the authorities and deported to Siberia, where they vanished without trace. The machinery of mass terror ran haywire, enmeshing thousands of innocents, ruining and embittering lives to no purpose.

The cruelties of the reign, in themselves essentially a continuation of Petrine policies, accentuated popular hatred against the Germans: oppression and injustice had been bad enough under Peter; under Germans they were intolerable, especially when the new nobility found itself no less vulnerable than the old nobility or the common people. The Volynsky affair of 1740 showed just why the regime inspired such fear and hatred. Volynsky, brilliant and energetic administrator and diplomat under Peter I, enjoyed great influence under Anna, becoming a member of the Cabinet in 1738. Here, however, he made the mistake of trying to curb the power of the Germans, and to restore and regularize the authority of the Russian nobility. He attempted to oust Bühren by an ill-conceived appeal to Anna against his misrule. Incensed by his denunciation of her favourite, Anna turned him over to Bühren himself who in turn delivered him to the Secret Chancery. Convicted after torture on a number of fictitious charges (including plotting to usurp the throne) he was beheaded after the severing of his tongue and right hand.

A long drawn-out and useless war against Turkey added to the unrelieved gloom of this sombre decade. Anna died at last in October 1740, bitter, disillusioned and unlamented. The next twelve months saw a round of furious power-struggles among the Germans. Dying childless, Anna named as her successor the two-month-old Ivan VI, son of her niece, the Princess of Brunswick. Bühren, hovering relentlessly over the deathbed, secured his own nomination as Regent, but his rule, surprisingly, lasted only three weeks, and he himself was overthrown by Münnich in a midnight counter-coup. So finally the hated Bühren, who had lorded it over Russia for ten years, was unceremoniously bundled off into exile. The Princess of Brunswick was named Regent in his place, with Münnich wielding the real power as her right-hand-man. Within a year, Münnich was ousted in turn by the sly and unsuspected Ostermann.

Empress Elisabeth and National Resurgence 1741–1762

This squalid round of plot and counter-plot came to an end in November 1741, with a *coup* in favour of Elisabeth, daughter of Peter I and Catherine I. Elisabeth had hitherto wisely kept out of politics and her claims to the throne had been ignored. In her early thirties, buxom, generous and warmhearted, she emerged as the ideal figurehead to oppose to the grim and hated Germans. Her appeal to the nobility and the Guards, after a decade of humiliation, was irresistible. Backed by a resolute clique (which included the ambassadors of France and Sweden, anxious for political reasons to terminate the rule of the Brunswicks),

Elisabeth appeared by night at the barracks of the Preobrazhensky regiment, and evoking her father's memory, appealed for support. Already well suborned, the Guards acclaimed her with enthusiasm, and escorted her in triumph to the Winter Palace. The Brunswick family were roused from their beds and packed off into exile, the infant Emperor being immured for life at Schlüsselburg. Ostermann and the other Germans were chased out of office and sent to Siberia.

Elisabeth's twenty-year reign has tended to be overshadowed by that of her more celebrated successor, Catherine II. Yet in some ways it stands comparison with credit. In contrast to the dour and shrewish Anna, Elisabeth brimmed with warmth, high spirits and *bonhomie*, was extremely sociable, and enjoyed the uninhibited company of peasants, gypsies and Cossacks as much as that of courtiers (one of her favourites, whom she married secretly, was a Ukrainian Cossack). Luxurious and pleasure-seeking ('not an ounce of nun's flesh about her'—remarked the British minister) she kept in the forefront of western fashion, danced the minuet to perfection, ran up astronomical bills with her Parisian dressmaker, and spared no expense to make St Petersburg the rival of Versailles. She was both sensual and devout, dashing contritely from her boudoir to her chapel, and making frequent pilgrimages to religious retreats. Apart from books of devotion and romantic French novels, she whiled away her time with cards, gossip, field sports, an incessant round of balls and masquerades, and an almost pathological gourmandizing, for she suffered agonies from boredom, restlessness and a basic insecurity. Like her father, she was notoriously short-tempered, flew into a rage over trifles, and swore like a trooper. But though she overreacted violently to imagined slights, she was quick to forgive, and with some rare exceptions at the beginning of her reign, was not vindictive or harsh.

Certainly, unlike Catherine, she was no intellectual, and her education left much to be desired. To the end of her days she believed that Britain was geographically joined to the continent. On the other hand, she inherited from both her parents a shrewd native wit which served her as well as any formal instruction. The hard school of experience, too, had taught her much, without, as with Anna, souring her disposition. She was a good judge of men, and made a point of selecting Russians rather than foreigners to high office: certainly, her ministers, Bestuzhev and Pyotr Shuvalov, were men of outstanding ability. Though she was notoriously slow to take decisions (as with Elizabeth of England, her delays and tergiversations in signing state-papers were the despair of her ministers), this perhaps stemmed less from indolence than from caution, and a natural and understandable desire to keep open all available options until the last possible moment. Her claim to be returning to the traditions of her father was meant sentimentally rather than literally. The fatigues of office frankly bored her, and she left the business of government to a small advisory council, later enlarged and established as the *Konferents*. But though self-indulgent and self-centred, Elisabeth was not frivolous, but genuinely anxious to do what seemed best for her country This was especially true of her foreign policy. If she attended the *Konferents* but rarely, she meditated on policy at her leisure, and once resolved on a course of action, gave her ministers full support and encouragement.

A start was made in several fields where Catherine II was later to reap the credit. In the area of codification, the criminal law was updated, and plans were laid for the overall discussion of legislative reform by a representative assembly. Cultural westernization was much intensified. Educated opinion was brought into contact with Enlightenment ideas, thanks partly to one of Elisabeth's favourites, the francophile Ivan Shuvalov, friend and correspondent of Voltaire, and known as 'the Russian Pompadour'. The career of Lomonosov showed how far the cultural gap between Russia and the west had narrowed since the time of Peter I. In foreign affairs, it was an age of triumph, Elisabeth's staunchness throughout the Seven Years' War contributing materially to Russia's success.

The *Konferents* was headed by Pyotr Shuvalov. The Shuvalov brothers, Pyotr and Alexander, had befriended Elisabeth in the years before her accession, and participated in the coup of 1741. Elisabeth trusted them implicitly (their cousin Ivan became her favourite), and placed Alexander in charge of the all-important Secret Chancery. To Pyotr, she virtually turned over control of domestic affairs for twenty years. Pyotr Shuvalov, though clever, enterprising and a masterly organizer, was avaricious and corrupt to a degree hitherto unprecedented. He brooked no criticism, browbeat the Senate and his colleagues on the *Konferents* and governed with arrogant self-assurance and audacity. He turned the nation's economy to his own private advantage, taking out monopolies in key industries for himself and his supporters, and using his official influence to suppress his competitors and pay off personal scores. But his numerous reform projects, however tainted with personal objectives, were intelligent, bold and effective, and helped to make the reign a time of new-found confidence and panache.

The problem of the succession, however, remained a running sore. In 1742, Elisabeth appointed as heir her nephew, the grandson of Peter I, Duke Peter of Holstein-Gottorp. Ill-bred, ill-educated and apparently mentally unbalanced, Peter was a drunken boor and poltroon who scoffed openly at the Church, played the fool at Elisabeth's funeral, and indulged an obsession for military uniforms and drills. His main characteristic, which he made no effort to conceal, was his scorn for Russia and all things Russian, and his hero-worship of the national enemy, Frederick II of Prussia. On his accession as Peter III in 1762, he outraged all sections of the nobility by terminating the war with Prussia on the very eve of final victory, and restoring to Frederick all Russia's hard-won conquests of the past seven years. He sealed his doom by his apparent intention to entrust the administration to a clique of favourites from Holstein. The Guards in particular were indignant at his plans to send the army against Denmark to fight for his private Holstein interests.

His young wife, Catherine, on the other hand, selected by Elisabeth from the minor German principality of Anhalt-Zerbst, did all she could to win popularity and support. Ambitious, winning, calculating and resourceful, she aspired with breathtaking boldness and skill to the throne itself. By 1757, she was busy plotting and building up her own party. The lessons of the age of palace-revolutions were not lost on her: she made certain of winning over the Guards, choosing her friends and lovers from among their number. In 1762, after six months of misrule by her husband, Catherine overthrew him in an armed *coup*. Forced to abdicate, Peter was soon afterwards murdered.

Imperial Government 1725–1762

The age of palace-revolutions is often seen as a period of abysmal decline, or a stagnant lull between the reigns of Peter I and Catherine II. Such a view is considerably overdrawn. Sensational as the revolutions were, their impact on government and policy was generally far less than was imagined outside Russia. Those who organized the revolutions, though representing rival factions, all belonged, after all, to the nobility. Their aim was to gain power and patronage, not to tamper with the machinery of government. Apart from the oligarchs of 1730, they never contemplated altering Russia's constitutional structure or redirecting her basic lines of policy; and the old nobility, after its rebuff in 1730, ceased to carry any independent weight. By mid-century, both old and new nobility formed a virtually united homogeneous class, firmly wedded to autocracy. The Table of Ranks continued to supply the army and bureaucracy with a regular flow of trained personnel, and formed a tough substructure which ensured basic continuity whatever the change of ruler. In any case, most of the czars and czarinas, especially before 1741, were mere figureheads, with little effective influence on policy. Policy-making was taken over by executive committees under able and experienced administrators: the Supreme Privy Council under Menshikov; the Cabinet of Ministers under Ostermann; and the *Konferents* under Bestuzhev and the Shuvalovs. All these men had served their apprenticeship under Peter I, and their rule reflected many of his aims and methods.

This absorption of power by tight executive committees was accompanied by a corresponding decline in the authority of the Senate and Colleges, which were drastically streamlined in the interests of economy and efficiency. The collegiate staff was slashed by half, and decision-making passed from the board-members to the president, himself often a member of the supreme ruling committee. The Senate was an early victim of retrenchment. Its traditional responsibility for the co-ordination of foreign affairs, the armed forces and finance, was taken over by the Supreme Privy Council, which sent its orders direct to the Colleges, bypassing senatorial discussion altogether. Stripped even of its role as chief court of appeal, the Senate sank into insignificance until Elisabeth's accession. Coming to power on a pledge of reviving her father's traditions, Elisabeth restored most of its former rights, though again, control of foreign, military and naval affairs was retained by the *Konferents*. The Senate under Elisabeth played an important role in supervising administration at collegiate and provincial level, and promoting finance and trade. It enacted much of the legislation of the reign. Nevertheless it remained firmly under the control of the *Konferents*, which carefully screened its membership and activities.

Provincial government also underwent considerable pruning. Already in Peter's last years, his ambitious provincial reforms had proved unworkable and the countryside had come under military rule. In 1727, his complex and costly apparatus of civilian government was abolished. The *voevoda*, with a much reduced staff and comprehensive powers,

E

was reinstated as supreme authority. Peter's abortive attempt to separate administrative and judicial functions was abandoned, the *voevoda* becoming supreme judge in his own province. Likewise, both municipal autonomy and the Chief Magistracy were discontinued, town government becoming the responsibility of the *voevoda*.

An institution which continued to function unimpaired was the Secret Chancery. Closed by order of the soft-hearted Catherine I, it was reopened by Anna in the panicky aftermath of 1730. But even when the immediate danger to the throne had subsided, it continued busily rooting out opposition. The reign of terror under Ushakov proved to be no temporary aberration; the Chancery continued to work at full pressure in Elisabeth's reign, under Alexander Shuvalov. In the first place, Anna's German ministers were hunted down, and subjected to humiliating show-trials as a prelude to banishment. In the second place, the Shuvalovs were no less zealous than Ushakov to suppress opposition among the masses: the number of ordinary people sent to Siberia at the instigation of Pyotr Shuvalov alone is put at 80,000. On her accession, Elisabeth swore never to sign a death-warrant, and in 1744, she formally abolished capital punishment. In the 1750s, however, with the revision of the criminal law, the number of capital offences was actually increased, particularly in the case of offences against property. At a time when the works of the *philosophes* were beginning to appear in Russia, it was decreed that for murder committed in the course of a felony, the culprit should be gibbetted from a hook inserted between the ribs. Several suggestions of this kind came from Elisabeth herself. For all her fondness for the common people, and for all that she was the daughter of Peter the Great, Elisabeth accepted that she owed her throne to the nobility, and made sure of consulting their interests at all times. Inquisitional methods, summary trials and penal savagery remained the essence of czarist rule.

The Church retained the role of dutiful servility to which Peter I had reduced it. It was in no position to exploit the palace-revolutions, and gave its blessing indiscriminately to each new occupant of the throne. Its lands and moneys were a standing temptation. During the Turkish Wars and Seven Years' War they were sequestered, nominally for the duration. Finally, under Peter III, all church properties were secularized outright, an act disavowed but later confirmed by Catherine II. Both Anna and Elisabeth practised a form of Orthodoxy that was close to bigotry; under Anna there was even an *auto-da-fé* at St Petersburg.

Ostermann and the Shuvalovs exploited this religiosity by despatching missionary expeditions to proselytize among the non-orthodox peoples, especially in Siberia and the border regions, in order to consolidate imperial rule.

The rigid standards of accountancy set by Peter I declined markedly after his death, despite administrative cutbacks. Expenditure on the armed forces and diplomatic service soared. Bounties and subsidies for allies were especially heavy, and the costs of the Seven Years' War were exorbitant. Budgetary difficulties were compounded by mounting court extravagance, rising imports of western luxuries, and the inability of an exhausted peasantry to pay its taxes which quickly fell into arrears. By 1733, there was a budgetary deficit, which grew to chronic proportions even before the Seven Years' War. The government searched around for remedies. The continuing use of the military to exact taxes by force, particularly under Anna, proved self-defeating. It led to mass peasant flights and still left the poll-tax in arrears. More ingenious approaches were tried by the enterprising Pyotr Shuvalov, who strove to diversify the sources of revenue by stimulating economic activity in the private sector. He leased out a variety of monopolies in industry and trade, increased the level of fluid capital by currency devaluations, and while uniting the Empire economically through the abolition of internal customs tariffs in 1754, gave protection to Russian industrialists by trebling import duties. At the same time, while striving to ease the peasant burden by the gradual replacement of direct taxes by indirect, Shuvalov raised the excise on salt and spirits. In spite of such measures, however, with the steep rise in military costs and the insatiable demand for luxury goods, the budgetary deficit leaped to eight million roubles by 1760, raising for the first time the spectre of a national debt.

Until recently it was supposed that the period was one of uniform economic decline. In fact, however, it is clear that despite some slackening in the first dozen years after 1725, the impetus given to trade and industry by Peter I was well maintained. The government continued at all times to satisfy the needs of the armed forces. Indeed, arms and munitions were now fully supplied by domestic production. The high quality of Russian weaponry, especially artillery, was clearly demonstrated in the Seven Years' War. The metallurgical industry in general, made striking advances. By 1762, the number of foundries had tripled since 1725, and iron production increased two-and-a-half times. As early as 1750, the Urals became Europe's leading iron-producing area, over-taking Britain and Sweden. New light industries catering for the home market also sprang up, such as glassware, leatherware and porcelain-ware. On the other hand, while exports continued to rise, the credit-balance was greatly narrowed by the steep rise in imported luxuries.

6

Russia as a European Power

Despite fainéant monarchs and palace-revolutions, there was no diminu-
tion of Russia's Great Power status, as her growing involvement in
European affairs makes clear. Her policy, which remained firmly
westward-looking and attuned to the concept of the balance of power,
was guided by two successive statesmen of rare foresight and skill, each
of whom had served his apprenticeship under Peter I: Ostermann and
Bestuzhev.

Ostermann and Consolidation 1725–1741

Ostermann had a useful background as chief negotiator at Aaland and
Nystadt. A German by birth, cautious, patient and meticulous, he held
that after the colossal strains of the long war with Sweden, Russia's
immediate need was for a breathing-space in which to assimilate her
gains. This her enemies were unwilling to grant. Each of them sought
to profit from her internal disorders in order to reverse her advances. A
sizeable Swedish faction, backed by France, conspired to regain the
Baltic provinces. Turkey, alarmed by Peter's incursion into Persia,
inspired frequent raids by the Crimean Tartars into the Ukraine. Relations with Warsaw were vexed by the problem of the Polish succession.

Ostermann aimed at protecting Russia's borders by peaceful diplomacy. The most experienced envoys were sent to Warsaw and Stockholm, laden with funds with which to foster parties friendly to Russia.
But Ostermann also recognized that to keep her enemies in check,
Russia must commit herself to one or other of the existing continental
alliances. Her most natural ally seemed to be Austria, also concerned
with events in Poland and Turkey; and in 1726 he concluded an Austro-
Russian alliance, the cornerstone of his system and a decisive influence

in Europe for the next forty years. Austria agreed to guarantee Russia's European borders and to assist her in the event of war with Turkey: Russia in return adhered to the Pragmatic Sanction.*

On the basis of the Austrian alliance, Ostermann built up a chain of lesser agreements to protect individual stretches of Russia's frontier. To check Sweden, he signed compacts with Prussia, Denmark and England (ending the recent tension in Anglo-Russian relations). To placate Turkey, he returned Peter's unassimilated gains on the Caspian. The Siberian and far-eastern frontiers he secured by a demarcation treaty with China.

Russia was protected in every quarter but one. Poland, weak and anarchic, represented the obvious spearhead of any invasion from the west. For Russia to lessen her control at Warsaw was to expose herself to attack. When, in 1733, the Polish throne fell vacant, France, in an effort to reassert her traditional influence at Warsaw, engineered the election of her own candidate Stanislas Leszczynski.† Ostermann took up the challenge without hesitation. For the first time since Peter's death, Russia went to war. Her troops poured into Poland to oust Leszczynski. At Danzig, where he had taken refuge, Russian troops clashed with French. Danzig fell to the Russians, Leszczynski fled to France and Russia's candidate was duly enthroned at Warsaw.

Thus far, Ostermann had an unbroken run of success at little cost. Either by skilful diplomacy or the timely use of force, he achieved his ends without involving Russia in any wider conflict. In 1735, however, when the French invaded Austrian territory, he was obliged to assist the Habsburgs by sending a diversionary force of 20,000 men to confront the French on the Rhine. This was the furthest west that Russian troops had yet been seen, and France quickly sued for peace. But while this *démarche* was certainly effective and impressive, it is questionable whether it really served Russian interests to pull Austria's chestnuts out of the fire. Furthermore, this was France's second humiliation by Russia in two years. The French plotted to bring about Ostermann's downfall, and incited Sweden and Turkey to take up arms again.

Indeed, French agitation at Constantinople led directly to a Russo-Turkish war in 1736. This signified the reversal of Ostermann's policy

---

* A decree of the Emperor Charles VI nominating his daughter Maria-Theresa as heir to the Habsburg dominions.
† Leszczynski, who had already ruled Poland briefly under Swedish protection, 1704–1709, was the father-in-law of Louis XV.

of containment. He advised against war; but his prudent counsels were overruled by the Empress Anna, backed by Bühren and Münnich. All three were confident of a lightning victory with Austrian help, which would avenge the Pruth disaster of 1711, sweep the Turks out of Europe, and revive the tarnished prestige of Anna and the German clique.

The war began with a series of costly triumphs under Münnich. The Crimea was quickly overrun. But the question of supplies was fatally mismanaged. Sickness was rife, and thousands perished of typhus. Furthermore, Münnich's failure to eliminate the Crimean Tartars turned the peninsula into a death-trap. Münnich's communications, and then his very army itself lay at the mercy of these elusive marauders, who finally compelled him to make a hasty retreat. The Crimea was evacuated. The cost of the initial victories, a tragically disproportionate 100,000 casualties, had been in vain. Austria, having rendered little effective aid, herself suffered defeat, and withdrew from the war, leaving Russia dangerously in the lurch.

To Ostermann fell the task of terminating this debacle. So desperate was Russia's plight, that when France offered herself as mediator, Ostermann gave her leave to secure peace for Russia at any price. The resulting Treaty of Belgrade (1739) was an almost total humiliation. After all her sacrifices, Russia's only gain was Azov, minus its fortifications; and even then her ships were still excluded from the Black Sea. To add insult to injury, Turkey maintained a stubborn refusal to recognize the Romanovs' imperial title.

The Treaty of Belgrade was Ostermann's ruin: for though he had opposed the war from the start, he was held responsible for its catastrophic outcome. His abortive bid for power in 1741 sealed his ruin, and he was an early victim of the anti-German reaction which accompanied the accession of Elisabeth.

In 1741, Sweden, at France's instigation, suddenly launched her cherished war of revenge, hoping to profit from the constitutional chaos at St Petersburg following Anna's death, and counting on Russia's continued imbroglio with Turkey. But Russia's forces were by now free to deal with this threat from the north; and any notion that her military strength had been sapped was decisively rebuffed. The Swedish invasion was halted and thrown back. It soon turned into a rout, the Swedes fleeing headlong into Finland, the Russians in close pursuit and overwhelming numbers. By the Treaty of Abo (1743), far from gaining her original object, Sweden was forced to cede the small province of Kymmenegard, north of Vyborg.

Bestuzhev and the Prussian Challenge 1741–1757

The accession of Elisabeth, though effected with French support, brought no advantage to France. Elisabeth and her ministers were resolved to brook no further interference from foreigners, German or French; and when the French ambassador demanded payment for his government's aid to Elisabeth in terms of a pro-French alignment, he was quickly sent packing. Elisabeth's policy was a revival of her father's tradition of sturdy independence and national glory.

The embodiment of the new outlook was her gifted chancellor, Bestuzhev. Opulent and pleasure-seeking, shrewd and brazenly corrupt, he admitted to taking bribes, but boasted that however much he accepted from Russia's allies, he was never in the pay of her enemies. With wide experience of European politics as a career diplomat, and exceptional foresight, Bestuzhev saw sooner than most that the immediate threat to Russia was no longer presented by Turkey, who was to remain quiescent for the next quarter-century—but by Prussia. For forty years good relations had existed between St Petersburg and Berlin: but on his accession in 1740, Frederick II had embarked on a policy of deliberate expansionism at the expense of Austria. At the beginning of Elisabeth's reign, many, including the empress, favoured neutrality, or even alliance with Prussia. It was Bestuzhev who succeeded in removing the scales from their eyes. Frederick's aggression, he pointed out, ultimately menaced Russia as much as Austria: his disturbance of the balance of power jeopardized the security of the Baltic provinces, which bordered East Prussia; and threatened to disturb the tranquillity of Sweden, Poland and Turkey. Bestuzhev's aim was to build up a coalition to contain Prussian expansion, by resuscitating the Austrian alliance and seeking an understanding with England. England, concerned as ever for Hanover, shared Bestuzhev's fears of Prussia, and in 1741 a defensive alliance was concluded. When Frederick invaded Saxony in 1745, Bestuzhev set in motion an impressive show of force, with the mobilization of troops in Courland, and a stern warning to Frederick to withdraw. The ploy succeeded, and peace was restored.

Bestuzhev realized, however, that the danger was by no means over and persuaded Elisabeth of the need to maintain an effective deterrent.

In 1746, he renegotiated the Austrian alliance for a period of twenty-five years. At the same time he concerted policing methods with England. Again, peace was concluded in 1748, this time for another eight years.

But within two years Frederick was already scheming to push Sweden into another invasion of Russia, and diplomatic relations between St Petersburg and Berlin were broken off. Bestuzhev was becoming convinced of the necessity of a preventive war to 'clip the King of Prussia's wings', as he put it. He insisted on an immediate increase in Russia's armed forces. By now he enjoyed the enthusiastic backing of the empress, not only stung to the quick by certain lewd innuendoes from Frederick, but fired by Bestuzhev's suggestion of crowning her father's achievements by the dismemberment of Frederick's kingdom and the annexation of East Prussia. Bestuzhev negotiated fresh agreements with Austria and England. Russian troops stood ready on the border of East Prussia.

Suddenly, in 1756, the alliance with England, the crux of Bestuzhev's system, collapsed. The notorious 'diplomatic revolution' set the traditional European alliance-system into reverse, when England, in a rapid *volte-face*, defected from the Austro-Russian camp in return for a non-aggression pact with Prussia. Elisabeth, outraged by what she saw as England's treachery, was all the more bent on destroying Frederick, and ordered the build-up of troops to continue. Meanwhile Bestuzhev concerted a plan of attack with Austria and rebuilt his system by a *rapprochement* with the traditional enemy, France, now moving into the Austrian orbit. By the end of 1756, as Russia, Austria and France concluded a series of offensive alliances, Frederick invaded Saxony in a bid to break out of encirclement. This *démarche* cemented the Franco-Russian compact, and war began.

The Seven Years' War 1757–1762

In 1757, the Russian army entered East Prussia and advanced on Tilsit. The first encounter came at Gross-Jägersdorf. For some time the issue was doubtful. Russian leadership was indecisive, while a massive enemy onslaught almost broke the Russian centre. Only a bold and unscheduled last-minute attack on the Prussian flank saved the day. The Prussians were routed, and the way lay open to Königsberg.

But a successful pursuit was hindered by events at St Petersburg. Elisabeth suffered a sudden stroke: should she die, the pro-Prussian

Grand Duke Peter was certain to reverse her policy. Bestuzhev, out to secure his own future, sent out secret orders that the victory at Gross-Jägersdorf was not to be exploited. The Russians withdrew from East Prussia, leaving Frederick free to inflict resounding defeats on France and Austria.

Elisabeth, however, unexpectedly recovered, to confront her chancellor's duplicity; and Bestuzhev was banished. The *Konferents* could ill afford the loss of his clear-headed and vigorous leadership. In addition to the empress' uncertain health, which continued to inhibit the war-effort, was the problem of the alliance: both France and Austria were dragging their heels. France's quarrel was with England rather than Prussia; while both France and Austria were increasingly fearful of Elisabeth's ambitions: the prospect of Russian expansion further west as the result of a successful war was even more alarming than the Prussian threat. Both complained of Russia's 'excessive influence', and plotted to confine her 'within her previous boundaries'.

It thus fell to Russia to bear the brunt of the war; and it was due partly to Elisabeth's own determination not to yield before final victory, that the ramshackle alliance survived. Russia's war aims, insisted Elisabeth, remained 'the essential and permanent crippling of the King of Prussia'.

In 1758, the Russians again overran East Prussia. Sweeping across Poland, they entered Pomerania and Brandenburg itself. At Zorndorf, near Küstrin, they met the Prussians under Frederick, in what proved to be Europe's bloodiest battle of the century. Frederick employed his notorious 'oblique' tactic,* which had seldom failed to roll up an enemy line. Unbelievably, the Russians stood firm in the face of murderous artillery fire. The outcome was doubtful: both sides claimed victory, while losing 20,000 men each. But though Frederick could claim to have checked the Russian advance, many more such 'victories' would ruin him.

In the 1759 campaign, the Russians took Frankfurt-on-the-Oder. Joined by the Austrians at Kunersdorf, they confronted Frederick once more. As at Zorndorf, Frederick's 'oblique' tactic failed him, and despite heavy losses, the Austro-Russian line held, and launched a devastating counter-attack. Under a shattering barrage of Russian

* A manoeuvre relying on the concentration of forces on one wing with the aim of outflanking the enemy, and—by a rapid change from column-formation to line-formation—rolling up his line.

artillery, the Prussian line broke and scattered, leaving 20,000 dead. Frederick himself barely escaped capture in what he rightly called 'that horrible catastrophe'. Kunersdorf was indeed the heaviest defeat of his career. Once again, however, news of Elisabeth's failing health prevented an immediate Russian follow-up.

The following year, Russia pushed on with a remarkable series of triumphs, taking temporary possession of Berlin itself. In 1761, a joint naval and military descent on Kolberg secured the heart of Prussia, and while Frederick contemplated suicide, the Russians prepared for a triumphant finale to the war. They were deprived of victory only by a freakish combination of circumstances. In the first place there were the habitual vacillations of the Austrians, for whose 'heaven-sent stupidity' Frederick had good cause to be grateful. Secondly, in December 1761 came the death of Elisabeth and the accession of Peter III. 'Heaven be thanked', exclaimed Frederick, 'our back is free.'

Almost the first of Peter's acts was to order an immediate cease-fire and to throw Elisabeth's policy into reverse. All the hard-won territory, the fruit of heavy casualties and crippling expense, was returned to Frederick without a single precondition. Abandoning the Austrians (he even sent detachments to assist Frederick against them), he concluded a formal alliance with Prussia.

Humiliating as Peter's policy was, Catherine II wisely agreed to let it stand. The main purpose for which Russia had gone to war, had, after all, been won: Frederick's ambitions had been checked and Prussian expansionism contained. Prussia no longer threatened Russian interests; on the contrary, Elisabeth's cherished dismemberment of Prussia would now be undesirable, since it would shift the balance of power in favour of France and Austria. Good relations with Prussia were therefore maintained. For his part, Frederick never forgot how close he had come to catastrophe, and friendship with Russia became an integral part of Prussian policy.

Russia's army, 400,000 strong, had shown itself to be one of the finest in Europe. Unlike most western armies, it was a national force, overwhelmingly Russian in composition, and despite indifferent leadership, its morale and resilience made a profound impression on western statesmen.

7

The Rise of the Nobility

The period 1725 to 1762 marks an important transition-stage in the evolution of the nobility. On the one hand there was the continuing formation of a stable professional bureaucracy, gaining improvements in its conditions of service. On the other hand there was a growing domination of the nobility in economic and social life. The squabbles between old and new nobles died down after 1730. Henceforth their interests were virtually indistinguishable: both enjoyed new social and cultural privileges; both prospered from the expanding possibilities of serf exploitation; both were united in seeking a relaxation of their duties to the state.

After Peter's death there was no longer a strong driving-force in the person of the autocrat. Favourites and committee-men rose to power, all nobles, with the interests of their class at heart; while a particularly decisive role was enjoyed by the noble Guards. Inevitably, the nobles as a class were now in a position to bargain and compromise with the autocrat, and to win concessions in return for their co-operation. In 1730, the nobility gave its collective guarantee to autocracy. In return, the autocrat recognized the need to make adjustments in its terms of employment. The implicit contract between autocrat and nobility was renegotiated on terms more favourable to the noble. Some relaxation of duties was inevitable: the strains imposed by Peter I were too onerous to survive him long; and in any case, once the crucial struggle with Sweden was over, the tasks ahead were relatively less strenuous. Common to the many petitions addressed to Anna in 1730 (in addition to assurances of loyalty) were pleas for reductions in the length of compulsory state-service, more frequent leaves-of-absence and repeal of the Entail law. Another request was for the founding of a military academy exclusively for nobles, so that the young serviceman could gain his commission without having to rub shoulders with the lower ranks.

The government duly took note of these requests. In 1731, Anna established the exclusive Noble Land Cadet Corps, and formally abolished the Entail law. In 1736, she agreed to reduce the maximum term of obligatory service from life to twenty-five years; and though Anna had to retract her offer on the outbreak of the Turkish War, Elisabeth was later able to renew it and even to permit a lower limit of twenty years. Even so, the plea was repeatedly made for a concession still more radical, namely that obligatory state-service be discontinued altogether. In 1762, this request, too was granted by Peter III in his *Manifesto concerning the Freedom of the Nobility*. The *Manifesto* declared that except in time of war, nobles were no longer legally bound to serve, though they were strongly urged to volunteer. They were free to retire to their estates or travel abroad without hindrance.

The significance of the *Manifesto* is sometimes missed. It did not represent, as might appear, a surrender by the autocrat to the nobility, a concession extorted under duress. Rather it constituted a formal decla-ration of the healthy state of the civil service. The bureaucracy was now so well staffed with trained professionals, that it could dispense with the expedient of obligatory conscription. This was not a reversal of the Petrine concept of service, but a recognition that service was no longer necessary in its original form. Indeed, the *Manifesto* not only insisted that service was still the métier of the noble, but stressed the importance of high educational standards. Its tone was selective: it demanded quality, not just mere numbers.

The *Manifesto* did not unleash a massive crop of resignations. Not only was the service still regarded as the only means to power and status; for the vast majority of the nobles it was the basis of their liveli-hood. Nothing, indeed, could be more misleading than to picture the typical noble as a wealthy, independent aristocrat, living off his rents and able to snap his fingers at state-service. It is reckoned that to earn an adequate income it was necessary to own at least 100 serfs. The percent-age of nobles with over 100 serfs was perhaps fifteen. Twenty-five per-cent owned between 20 and 100; while some sixty percent of nobles, the overwhelming majority, owned less than 20, and thus remained almost wholly dependent on state-service. Not even the more affluent nobles could dispense with state patronage. Enjoyment of a western style of life led to rising expenditure. Many families ennobled by Peter I went bankrupt; many others sought state assistance; and in 1754, at the instigation of Pyotr Shuvalov, a state-sponsored Bank of the Nobility was founded. Loans were repayable in the form of lands and serfs, and a growing number of estates became mortgaged to the government.

Under Elisabeth, there was increasing interest among nobles in the possibilities of industry. Pyotr Shuvalov was instrumental in transferring a large number of state-enterprises into private hands, notably in metallurgy and the cloth and liquor industries. The noble was attracted to industry by the prospect of greater profits than he could hope to gain from his state-salary or agriculture alone. Vodka-distilling and the manufacture of linen were especially popular, since they could be run on the estate with minimal overheads. The state continued to offer heavy financial backing and to indemnify the entrepreneur by placing wholesale orders, and even, at Shuvalov's insistence, by repurchasing its own factories at a loss!

As the nobleman's relations with the government were gradually readjusted to the satisfaction of both, the position of the bonded serf deteriorated. Firstly, there was a marked drop in the peasant population, which within a dozen years of the death of Peter I, declined by approximately two million. Part of this loss is attributable to the fearful losses of the Turkish War; part to the Secret Chancery, which caught up tens of thousands and spirited them off to Siberia. Untold thousands were also missing as a result of mass flights to border regions or abroad.

Secondly, there was a marked and rapid decline in the serfs' juridical status. Two processes were at work here. On the one hand, the state gradually absolved itself of responsibility for the well-being of the serf by depriving him of any vestige of juridical identity or civil rights. On the other hand, having completely disfranchized him, it surrendered him into the keeping of the noble. In 1727, the serf was specifically forbidden to seek employment in government service. The Table of Ranks was closed to him. No matter how talented he might be, he was excluded from participation at any level in the running of the country. In 1741, he was deprived of the customary right to swear allegiance to the sovereign; and was thus no longer considered a citizen or in any sense a concern of the state.

A series of laws bound him more tightly to the will of the noble. In 1730, he was deprived of the right to own land in his own name. In 1732, he could be transferred from one part of the country to another without warning. In 1736, a fugitive serf could be punished in whatever manner the noble thought fit. In 1747, a serf could be sold without hindrance, particularly as a recruit to the army. At the same time, however, he was debarred from volunteering for military service, as had been permitted under Peter I. The penalty for disobedience here was hard labour for life. In 1760, the noble was empowered to exile serfs to Siberia, and though he was not supposed to separate man and wife, nothing prevented him from separating parents and children. Further, for each serf thus exiled, the state offered financial compensation, the main purpose behind this scheme being the colonization of Siberia.

The tax-burden also increased. As in Peter's last years, military expeditions were sent out to the countryside to extort the taxes by force. This was especially prevalent under Anna. In the 1750s, taxation was increased on salt and spirits, by which the peasants, as the chief consumers, were hardest hit.

The growing harshness of peasant life is reflected in the growing incidence of mass flights, which tripled between 1730 and 1750. Peasants fled to Poland and the Baltic provinces, to the Urals, the Caucasus, the steppeland of the south and south-east, and the upper reaches of the Volga. Often they took to the forests, forming guerilla bands, sometimes led by army deserters and equipped with muskets and even cannons. Unrest was particularly rife among serfs working in factories and on Church lands; while to all the motives of discontent which the Russian peasant had, the non-Russian could add religious persecution. Inflamed by enforced proselytization, (which followed in the wake of colonization) the Mordvins and Bashkirs rose several times under Anna and Elisabeth. A peculiarly Russian phenomenon was the resurgence of 'Pretenders,' claiming to bring freedom in the name of the czar. Traditionalist by nature, the Russian peasant continued to see the czar as the father of his people; responsibility for their hardships lay not with him, but with his wicked advisers—the nobles. After the *Manifesto* of 1762 peasant unrest gained new impetus: now that the noble was emancipated from state service, what justification could there be for their own thralldom? When nothing happened to ease their plight, rumour spread that the czar had been suppressed by the nobles (as indeed, he had). Disturbances flared up again across the country, and the army was everywhere called in. Most rebellions were rapidly quelled, though some persisted for two or three years. But unrest was endemic in the countryside; violence simmered continuously below the surface.

8

St Petersburg Culture

The state continued to maintain a close check on the educational standards of the nobility. Under regulations laid down in 1736, instruction was to begin at the age of seven, with examinations at twelve, sixteen and twenty. The state-organized military academies did their work well, producing a regular supply of qualified officers and administrators.

Where education now differed was in its increasing social selectiveness. While Peter I had tried to offer careers open to all on the basis of merit, the nobility now saw to it that in education as elsewhere, the doors to promotion were closed to all but their own number. The Naval Academy, which under Peter had produced numerous graduates of non-noble birth, was reopened in 1752 as the Naval Cadet Corps, an establishment reserved exclusively for nobles. The Artillery and Engineering Academies suffered a similar fate. Most exclusive of all such institutes was the Land Cadet Corps, founded in 1731 for youths of the nobility and modelled by Münnich on the German *Ritterakademien*. Side by side with its vocational and functional aims, the Cadet Corps offered an aristocratic flavouring in the form of broader accomplishments and social polish. Courses were taught not only in mathematics and the military sciences, but also in languages, history, geography and jurisprudence. Recreational activities included riding, fencing, dancing, *belles-lettres* and amateur dramatics. The Cadet Corps enjoyed the prestige of a select finishing-school, an amalgam of Eton and Sandhurst.

With the waning of Peter I's 'cipher-schools', responsibility for primary education devolved increasingly on the army and church. Garrison-schools, set up under the auspices of the army, were the mainstay of elementary education in the provinces. While the church continued to offer general instruction through its parish-schools, its theological academies at Moscow, Kiev and elsewhere offered a rudimentary secondary schooling in the shape of a smattering of Latin, German, French and moral philosophy. Inadequate as such studies might seem, graduates of the seminaries frequently reached high office.

The Academy of Sciences fulfilled many of its founder's expectations. Through the publication of its learned *Commentarii*, it soon won a place among Europe's leading research-institutes, attracting to its ranks such outstanding western *savants* as Daniel Bernoulli and Leonhard Euler. The first issue of the *Commentarii* (1728) featured articles on differential calculus, a far cry from the schoolroom rudiments of Magnitsky's *Arithmetic*. Under Anna, indeed, the Academy tended to become the preserve of German professors, and its scholarly atmosphere was enlivened by raucous squabbles between German and Russian academicians. On the other hand, the Academy was less socially exclusive than most of the educational institutes; indeed all Russian academicians of the century, notably Lomonosov, were non-noble. Under Elisabeth, Russian scholars produced outstanding original work in mathematics and the sciences; while the Academy's practical usefulness—its second main function—showed itself in numerous studies of the geography, ethnography and natural resources of Russia. In 1745, it published the first accurate *Atlas of the Russian Empire*. In 1755, at the instigation of Lomonosov and Ivan Shuvalov, the University of Moscow was founded, in response to the dearth of professionals, particularly in the arts, economics and law. Significantly, provision was made for the admission of non-nobles. The University, however, made slow progress at first; it did not offer, as did the Cadet Corps, automatic promotion in the Table of Ranks, and German scholars long predominated on the faculty.

An important catalyst to the spread of letters and knowledge was the growth of printing presses. These sprang up at the Academy of Sciences, Moscow University, the Cadet Corps, and the College of War. Moscow University began publication of the twice-weekly *Moscow News*, a journal vastly more informative than its jejune namesake and forerunner. In 1759, Russia's first literary journal, Sumarokov's *Busy Bee*, appeared at St Petersburg. The Academy was a prolific source of learning, with its own press, bookshop and library. It put out the *St Petersburg News*, and under Lomonosov's editorship, began publication of *Monthly Articles*, a periodical purveying, in the form of translations

F

or original essays, the elements of contemporary science and enlightenment.

The 1730s saw the birth of a modern secular literature, modelled
closely on western pseudo-classicism. The Father of Russian letters was
the westernized and erudite Kantemir. Kantemir was instrumental in
the restoration of autocracy in 1730, and became ambassador at London
and Paris. In his satires, redolent of Boileau, he lauded the achievements
of Peter I as triumphs of reason and science, and mocked the ignorance
and obscurantism of the unenlightened, especially the clergy. Kantemir
was a purveyor of culture, an enlightener, rather than a truly creative
writer. In the commentaries which he appended to his satires, and in his
annotated translation of Fontenelle's *Entretiens sur la pluralité des mondes*,
he introduced the Russian reader to the Scientific Revolution and to
the canons of classical and modern literature.

The brightest luminary in the intellectual, cultural and scientific life
of mid-century Russia was Lomonosov. Hefty, bearlike, bluff and can-
tankerous, Lomonosov was a scholar of truly encyclopedic range, with
a fertile and original brain, equally at home in the sciences and the
humanities. A scientific genius in his own right, he was Russia's first
savant to win international renown for his work in electricity, atmo-
spherics and metallurgy. As the Grand Cham of Russian letters, the Dr
Johnson of St Petersburg, he pioneered the course of *belles-lettres*, laying
down singlehanded rules of grammar, style and versification, which he
exemplified in his own writings. His *Russian Grammar* (1744) soon
established itself as a classic. Lomonosov glowed with the buoyant
optimism of an Augustan deist: he acclaimed every sign of material
progress, and looked forward to the triumph of rationalism and science.
His two dignified odes *On Divine Majesty* reflect his faith in the orderly
Leibnizian chain of being, manifest in the immutable glories of nature.
Well-known is his eloquent obituary of Rikhman, the Academy's first
martyr to science, electrocuted while carrying out an experiment on
lightning. Cosmopolitan in his breadth of learning, Lomonosov was at
the same time a doughty patriot, insisting that Russia was now the
cultural equal of the west, and lambasting the arrogance of his German
colleagues. Not only was Lomonosov a guiding spirit behind the
foundation of Moscow University; he was, in his own person, as
Pushkin said, 'Russia's first university'.

In culture and outward appearance, the St Petersburg noble of the
mid-century bore little resemblance to his Muscovite grandfather or

even to his father. His formative years at the Cadet Corps (or sometimes under a foreign tutor), accustomed him to gentlemanly manners and accomplishment (a further edition of the *Honourable Mirror of Youth* appeared in 1740). Foreign travel, for example, as part of the occupation-forces in the Baltic provinces and East Prussia during the Seven Years' War, brought him face-to-face with western life. The example of the courts of Anna and Elisabeth and the import on a massive scale of the *agrémens* of western life—its art, furnishings, cuisine, wines, music and dance whetted his appetite for the aristocratic *douceur de vivre*.

Theatrical life took root. It began with amateur productions by pupils of the Cadet Corps, patronized by Elisabeth. In 1748, the cadets performed Voltaire's *Zaïre;* and in the following year Russia's first classical tragedy, *Khorev*, by Sumarokov. French and Italian repertory troupes were soon playing to enthralled audiences; opera and ballet became the rage; and in 1756 the first state theatres in Russia were founded at both capitals by imperial decree. In 1757, at the promptings of Ivan Shuvalov, an Academy of Fine Arts was founded at St Petersburg. Even freemasonry secured a foothold, though as yet it was mainly a modish diversion for the St Petersburg bloods, an excuse for tippling and roistering.

For Anna and Elisabeth, the architectural styles of Peter I, with their Dutch sobriety and heavy baroque grandeur, had begun to pall. Rastrelli the Younger catered for a lighter mood with an exuberant rococo, combining traditional Russian themes with the decorative frivolity of Dresden and Vienna. Rastrelli designed the magnificently ornate palaces of Peterhof and Czarskoe Selo, the wedding-cake extravaganzas of the Smol'ny Cathedral (where Elisabeth retired for periodic repentance), with its five burnished 'muscovite' cupolas; and the second Winter Palace, with its florid colonnades, intricate wrought-ironwork, and dramatic statuary.

At the capital and on his estate the noble strove to mirror the styles of his western counterpart. Many nobles now literally declined to speak the same language as their serfs, French being the accepted language of the court under Elisabeth. The gruff sergeant-major of the reign of Peter I gave way to the Elisabethan *petit-maître*, connoisseur of the sweet life. Even the coarsest country-squire in a remote backwater, with his dozen serfs, sported some form of distinctive 'European' dress and spoke of his peasants as 'canaille'.

In this aping of foreign modes and rage for all things French there was of course much foppery and dilettantism, as Kantemir, Sumarokov and other writers were at pains to point out. At the same time the period did see the first generation of a truly educated elite. The political writings of the time reflect the growing influence of the nobility. Autocracy remains the accepted basis of government; but emphasis shifts from Prokopovich's insistence on the monolithic authority of the autocrat to the equal importance of the nobility as co-partners in the task of bringing progress and enlightenment. Blending tradition with contemporary Enlightenment thought, Volynsky, Kantemir, Tatishchev and Lomonosov all stressed the benefits to the state of the partnership of absolutism and nobility and urged broader representation of the nobility in government. All argued staunchly in favour of serfdom as the basis of the economic supremacy of the nobility—and hence the well-being of Russia. Not even Lomonosov—himself the son of a peasant—disputed its necessity. Kantemir's satires aimed not at undermining the nobility but at purging it of sloth, ignorance and barbarism.

III

THE AGE OF CATHERINE THE GREAT

1762-1796

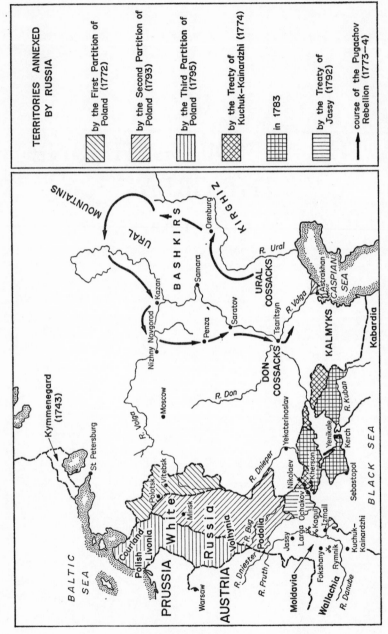

TERRITORIES ANNEXED
BY RUSSIA

by the First Partition of
Poland (1772)

by the Second Partition of
Poland (1793)

by the Third Partition of
Poland (1795)

by the Treaty of
Kuchuk–Kainardzhi (1774)

in 1783

by the Treaty of Jassy (1792)

course of the Pugachov
Rebellion (1773–4)

3. Russia's westward expansion under Catherine II and the course of the Pugachov Rebellion.

9

Catherine II and 'Enlightened Absolutism'

So artfully did Catherine deck her rule with the trappings of 'enlightened absolutism', that historians are hard put to sort myth from reality. How did a German upstart and usurper, without a drop of Russian blood in her veins or the shadow of a title to the throne, come to reign for thirty-four years as one of Russia's most successful and celebrated rulers? Unbounded willpower, ambition and lust for acclaim seem to have been her basic motives: '*Je veux terriblement ce que je veux,*' she confessed. These desires were backed by sparkling intelligence, energy, boldness and exceptional personal magnetism. Lacking the good looks of Elisabeth, Catherine more than made up for them with her captivating, though somewhat disingenuous charm. More calculating, more self-controlled than Elisabeth, she used her femininity with shrewd deliberateness. Her method, she avowed, was always to please: to be polite, gracious and sympathetic on principle; and to cultivate anyone who might prove useful. Her enemies she tried to win over with a show of magnanimity: bloodshed was always a last resort, though if necessary, she struck ruthlessly. As a rule, though, she preferred to kill with kindness: the golden handshake was much more to her taste than the stab in the back.

Catherine prided herself on her superior intellect: and certainly, in breadth of interests and cultivation, she far surpassed her immediate predecessors. As Grand Duchess, she had found consolation for her boorish husband not merely in dalliance, but by immersing herself in the works of the Enlightenment: Locke, Bayle, Montesquieu, Buffon, the Encyclopedists, and above all, Voltaire, were at her fingertips; and while by no means an original thinker, she shared and reflected the Enlightenment outlook, its lively humanism and faith in the efficacy of education, science, culture and law. She was no radical: 'I am an aristocrat,' she declared, 'it is my duty and my profession'. She mistrusted Rousseau's emotionalism and banned his *Emile* as unwholesome. 'Instinctively,' she said of the French Revolution, 'I feel the greatest contempt for popular movements of all kinds.' Rather, she saw herself in the role of 'enlightened despot', a notion which she spread across Europe through her assiduous cultivation of the *philosophes*. Voltaire was her 'master'; Montesquieu her 'breviary'; the *Encyclopédie* she could not dispense with 'for a single day'. This kind of treatment soon had many of the *philosophes* paying homage to her greatness: for them she was the 'Semiramis of the North', 'our' Catherine; 'she united' said Diderot, 'the soul of Brutus and the charms of Cleopatra,' '*C'est du Nord aujourd'hui que nous vient la lumière!*' exclaimed Voltaire.

Although much of this was mere flummery on Catherine's part, her respect for Enlightenment ideals in themselves was genuine enough. But she was no doctrinaire: her basic aim was simply to stay in power, to rule as 'enlightened despot' if possible, but to rule at all costs. She knew that whatever her prestige in the west, her position at home was fraught with dangers. There were plots to replace her by the ex-Czar Ivan VI or by her own son, Paul, ever resentful of her usurpation. There was a scheme to control her through a body reminiscent of the Supreme Privy Council. There were the Guards; as Catherine wryly observed: 'Every guardsman, when he looks at me, can say: "I made that woman"'; and no one knew better than she how easily the Guards could unmake what they had made. Then there were those special guardsmen, the Favourites, some of whom showed signs of political ambition. To immunize herself against these very real threats, Catherine exerted her extraordinary talents towards transforming herself into a living legend, a being seemingly above the humdrum of day-to-day politics, a presiding spirit, a *dea ex machina* come to save Russia from the squalor of the age of palace-revolutions and inaugurate the Golden Era. She became, in the words of Joseph II, '*la princesse de Zerbst Catharinisée*'.

She played her role with consummate art. Though a far more pure-blooded German than Anna or Peter III—Potyomkin used to mimic her accent—she took care not to repeat their errors, descanting at all times on her devotion to Russia. She posed as the spiritual daughter of Peter I. One echo of this was her assumption—only six years after her *coup d'état*—of the title 'Catherine the Great'; another—the famous

X Catherine the Great by S. Torelli.

(Russian State Museum, Leningrad)

XI Catherine II celebrates the victory of Chesme by A. Huehne.

XIII The Gibbet.
(*The British Museum*)

XIV Portrait of Pugachov superimposed on a
portrait of Catherine II.

Chesme.

XV Nicholas Ivanovitch Novikov
(*Radio Times Hulton Picture Library*)

XVII Mademoiselle Nelidova, a pensionnaire
at the Smol'ny Institute, by Levitsky.

XVI Beggars by I. A. Yermenev.

equestrian statue of Peter which she commissioned from the sculptor Falconnet. On its base was inscribed: '*Petro Primo—Catharina Secunda*'. A third echo of Peter's grandeur was her dazzingly successful foreign policy.

In imitation of Elisabeth, she displayed great veneration for the Church. Though privately a sceptic, who enjoyed jesting with Voltaire on matters religious, she took care to be seen regularly at her devotions, showed keen interest in shrines and relics, sat through her coronation-service with every appearance of piety, and ascribed her accession to God rather than to the Guards. St Petersburg was well worth a mass. None of this, however, stopped her from secularizing church property.

Catherine had a nice eye for stagecraft. She consciously set out to make her court a splendidly extravagant backdrop to her actions, and lavished on it a cool thirteen percent of her annual budget. The effects were stupendous: even blasé western diplomats rubbed their eyes in amazement. Wherever Catherine appeared, she always stood in the limelight, radiating queenly serenity amid a blaze of diamonds and adulation. She basked in flattery, while affecting to despise it, and kept unpleasant realities well out of sight. Her triumphal tour of the south in 1787 became proverbial for tinsel brilliance concealing sordid truths.

Much of her policy consisted of unacknowledged borrowings from her recent predecessors, to whose memory she did scant justice. The Russian Enlightenment, which flowered under her patronage, had taken root under Elisabeth. Her legislative and administrative reforms stemmed from plans mooted by the Shuvalovs. Her foreign policy was grounded in the military superiority won in the Seven Years' War. Above all, her social policy was shaped by that of the preceding forty years.

Catherine's outlook hardened under pressure of events. Her faith in human rationality was blighted by the Legislative Commission and shaken by the Pugachov rebellion. In the 1770s, she turned to institutional reform, pinning her hopes on good laws and wise administrators. But she was wary of going too far, and what she could not bestow from above she would not allow to be snatched from below. By 1790, her chief concern was simply to hold fast: alarmed by the French Revolution, she reverted to authoritarianism and hatchetmen. In the final analysis, beneath all the glitter, her policies turned out to be a surprisingly old-fashioned and sterile *étatisme:* the maintenance of order at home and grandeur abroad.

Autocratic Centralism

Catherine ruled as well as reigned. Though generous of her person, she was jealous of her power, and brooked no interference from her well-known succession of Favourites. Apart from Potyomkin, whose administrative genius was invaluable to her, she usually confined their activities to the boudoir. As one of them complained: 'I was nothing but a kept woman'. Whatever her private foibles, Catherine ruled with manly energy (*Catherine le Grand*, the *philosophes* dubbed her). She herself was the heart and soul of her government. Informed, intelligent, methodical and hardworking, she ruled the Empire from her study at the Winter Palace. She was advised by a small Imperial Council of select members of the *Generalitet*, supplemented by occasional *ad hoc* commissions. Schemes raised by her foreign minister, Panin, for a permanent executive body, she quietly shelved as detrimental to her power. From rule by committee, she reverted to personal autocracy.

Her right-hand-man and intermediary was the capable, self-effacing Procurator-General, Vyazemsky, whose authority now became all-encompassing. An amalgam of prime minister, home secretary, chancellor of the exchequer and attorney-general, he conferred daily with Catherine and passed on her instructions to the College presidents and provincial governors, whose activities he kept under continual surveillance through his staff of procurators.

Catherine abolished the now moribund collegiate system, replacing it in fact if not in name by a series of ministries, each under a president directly answerable to the Procurator-General. Each College was divided into separate departments, the heads of which met rarely and were responsible only to the president. Several Colleges were closed down. Most were made redundant by the provincial reforms of 1775. Only the 'first three Colleges' (Foreign Affairs, War, and the Admiralty) remained intact.

The powers of the Senate were also drastically curtailed. Catherine saw the Senate as an obstacle to autocratic centralization and feared the ambitions of Panin and his sympathizers to make it a focus for constitutional opposition. In 1763, she diluted its authority by splitting it into six departments (two in Moscow, four in St Petersburg). She retained it as supreme court of justice and formal overseer for provincial government, but transferred its original and main responsibility—the co-ordination of national policy—to the Imperial Council, and in particular to the Procurator-General.

The Church

In 1762, when Peter III decreed the secularization of church property, the Church still owned one-seventh of all serfs in Russia. Privately, Catherine approved of secularization; but she exploited the reaction which it provoked in order to ease herself into power as the protector of Orthodoxy, and duly revoked the decree. However, once in control, she determined to reimpose it, and found widespread disorders among ecclesiastical serfs a convenient excuse to do so (1764). A million church serfs now passed under state control, for the most part swelling Catherine's reserve of farewell gifts for unwanted Favourites and politicians; and most of the quitrent now paid by the serfs to the state went straight into her privy purse. Nearly two-thirds of Russia's monasteries were closed down. With secularization, the subordination of church to state was complete. The Bishop of Rostov, who ventured to protest, was unfrocked and gaoled for life. He was an exception: most ecclesiastics maintained a prudent silence, anxious to curry imperial favour and acquire positions on the Synod. A latter-day Prokopovich emerged in the person of Platon Levshin, whose unusual respect for science and enlightenment raised him to favour as court preacher, Archbishop, and later Metropolitan of Moscow. As ever, the Church was called upon to sermonize the peasantry into docile submission. The Archbishop of Kazan publicly excommunicated Pugachov in 1773. As head of the Church, Catherine was able to put at least one Enlightenment precept into action by calling a halt to religious persecution. In particular, the Old Believers were no longer obliged to pay twice the normal tax. But for them, as for many non-Orthodox, this relief came too late, as the Pugachov rebellion was to show.

Experiments in Enlightenment 1766–1768

In 1766, Catherine announced the establishment of a so-called *Commission for the Drawing-up of a New Code of Laws*, at which elected representatives of the nobility, the towns and the central organs of government were to convene in Moscow the following year. Historians differ as to Catherine's precise intentions. These were probably several, since she invariably kept more than one iron in the fire. In the first place, the Commission is to be seen as a highly successful publicity-stunt, in which Catherine courted popular approval by inviting public co-operation in an important piece of statecraft. The Commission added to her lustre and set the seal on her acceptance. She conducted the opening ceremonies in person and with all her customary flair, graci-ously accepting the title 'Great, All-wise and Mother of the Fatherland.' Secondly, her policy can be construed as a bid to broaden the base of her support, by appealing over the heads of the Guards, the *Generalitet* and the court camarillas, to the provinces and towns beyond. Thirdly, the Commission was the latest of several attempts (the most recent under Elisabeth) to tackle the long-standing problem of Law reform.

To sound opinion among the nobility as to how far her enlighten-ment ideas might be acceptable as a basis for reform, Catherine pub-lished her *Nakaz* or *Instruction for the Commission*. Catherine was justly proud of the *Nakaz*, into which she had put two years' hard work, though, as she was the first to admit, it was by no means original, most of its ideas being lifted from Montesquieu, Beccaria and the German cameralists. The *Nakaz* was a blueprint of enlightened absolutism, recommending that progress could best be realized within the frame-work of a *Rechtsstaat*, where the rights and duties of each citizen were clearly defined and guaranteed. Catherine insisted that autocracy should remain intact, but justified it on grounds of public expediency as the only workable form of government in an empire so vast. The main-spring of public life should shift, however, from state coercion to voluntary co-operation between autocrat and nobility.

The *Nakaz* was an advanced work for its time, too advanced, per-haps, for Russia. It was banned in France (a further boost to Catherine's reputation) and was hailed by Voltaire as 'the finest document of our time'. At her advisers' insistence, Catherine modified her early drafts (containing hints at the possible abolition of serfdom)—and circulation of the *Nakaz* was restricted to the upper echelons of the civil service. Even so, it was Russia's first essay in self-evaluation, and its appeal to natural law and utilitarian ethics, its call for judicial reform, humani-tarian penal legislation, social welfare and the rule of law were to provide considerable food for thought among educated Russians.

For the moment, however, the *Nakaz* remained suspended in limbo;

and the Commission, despite hopes that it might become a permanent representative and legislative assembly, turned out to be a nine days' wonder. After the initial pomp and ceremony—which served Catherine's purpose very effectively—interest and attendance faded. The formal plenary sessions and subcommittee debates to discuss particular problems degenerated into acrimonious squabbles between nobles and merchants on the question of serf-ownership. The meetings dragged on half-heartedly for eighteen months, until in 1768, on the outbreak of war with Turkey, Catherine prorogued the Commission. Ostensibly this was for the duration: but the Commission was not reconvened and the code of laws remained incomplete for the next sixty years.

State Security

The Secret Chancery (renamed 'Secret Expedition'), nominally abolished by Peter III, was quietly reopened by Catherine within six months of her accession. Whatever her private qualms, she could not dispense with this traditional bastion of autocracy. It was an important safeguard against noble intriguers, ambitious guardsmen and peasant *jacqueries;* while ever at the back of her mind was the threat of a bid for power by Paul. Catherine closely followed the Chancery's proceedings, entrusting them to Vyazemsky and later to the brutal Sheshkovsky, worthy successor to Ushakov and Alexander Shuvalov, and an expert in third-degree interrogations. Though Catherine denied that torture was used, Sheshkovsky and his tormented victims knew better. Hundreds of suspected critics of the regime were brought in for questioning in the 1760s and 1770s; and there were also important special inquiries: to investigate an attempt to release ex-Czar Ivan VI from Schlüsselburg (according to standing orders, the hapless Czar was murdered by his gaolers (1764)); to assess opposition among the clergy after the affair of the Bishop of Rostov (1764); to enquire into rioting at Moscow during an outbreak of plague (1771); and above all, to discover the causes of the Pugachov rebellion; on this occasion some 20,000 suspects passed through the Chancery's hands (1774).

The last years of the reign, especially after the French Revolution, saw a sharp reaction against Enlightenment ideas and intellectual freedom. Sheshkovsky and his minions were now kept busy as literary gendarmes, sifting through books, manuscripts and private correspondence. An index of forbidden works was compiled which included

Voltaire, Diderot, and most other *philosophes*. Freemasonry came under deep suspicion; but the chief victims of repression were social critics, notably Novikov and Radishchev, both of whom suffered at the hands of Sheshkovsky.

Provincial Reform

Provincial government was a chronic weak spot, as Catherine discovered for herself in the course of several tours across the Empire. Russia's sheer enormity and the daunting backwardness of provincial life gave her food for thought. The cutbacks made in 1727 had left the provinces dangerously undermanned in view of ever-mounting peasant unrest. In the vast *guberniya* of Kazan, for example, there were only eighty regular officials to control a population of two-and-a-half million. During the Pugachov rebellion, local authority crumbled. At her leisure, Catherine chewed over the minutes of the Legislative Commission, where nobles had complained of violence and lawlessness across the country. She pored over the writings of western jurists, notably Blackstone. She consulted with experienced administrators, and thrashed out solutions with the Imperial Council. The fruits of her labours were the Provincial Statute (1775) and Municipal Charter (1785).

In 1775, the administrative map was redrawn yet again. This time the Empire was divided according to density of population into fifty new *gubernii* of 800,000 inhabitants each. Each *guberniya* was subdivided into districts of 60,000 inhabitants. (The former *provintsii* were abolished.) In charge of the *guberniya* was the Governor—(sometimes two or three *gubernii* were entrusted to a Governor-General or Viceroy). The governor was the linch-pin of the whole system. He was hand-picked for loyalty, good sense and initiative; he took his orders direct from the Empress through the Procurator-General, and no longer from the Colleges and Senate; for although theoretically he was still accountable to the Senate, in fact he was answerable only to the Empress. In practice, his freedom of action was unlimited. All military units in the province lay at his disposal, and his word was law. Within his *guberniya*, he ruled as absolutely as the Empress. In the new southern provinces, Potyomkin lorded it like an independent monarch.

There was a massive decentralization of functions. Provincial affairs were removed from the Colleges at St Petersburg (which were gradually phased out) and redistributed among special local boards. Two boards controlled administration, finance and industry. Another, the so-called Public Welfare Board, took charge of schools, hospitals and almshouses. The judicial system was completely overhauled. Two boards were made responsible for civil and criminal justice, and below these was erected a triple hierarchy of separate courts for nobles, town-dwellers and state peasants.

The local nobility (and to a lesser extent the merchants) were also brought into the workings of local government. Certain posts were open to election on a class basis; in particular, that of marshal of the nobility (one for each province and district), the official spokesman for noble interests; and the *kapitan-ispravnik*, who was formal head of district administration. Certain magisterial posts were also open to election.

Despite appearances, however this did not mean local self-government or true decentralization of power. The Assemblies of the Nobility were not western Diets: there was no question of their putting pressure on the Governor. On the contrary, the Governor always had the last word: it was he who convened the elections, screened the candidates, and confirmed (or rejected) their election. In any case, few of the elective posts commanded prestige. Only the marshal of the nobility could begin to compare with the Governor in dignity, and his prestige was social rather than political. For the rest, the elected officials were held in some contempt. They performed minor functions, received much lower salaries than the professionals, and once elected, became mere auxiliaries of the Governor and his staff, who, as a contemporary observed, 'bent and twisted them like a pliant willow'. Furthermore, elective posts did not confer promotion in the Table of Ranks. The ambitious noble continued to enter the professional service.

Provincial administration was completed by the Municipal Charter (1785) which extended participation in government to selected town-dwellers. Owners of town property were divided into six classes, headed by the nobility and merchants (the latter subdivided into three 'guilds'). Each class elected a representative to sit on a six-man town council, or *duma*, which in turn elected a mayor. Here again, however, appearances were deceptive. In practice, control still rested with the Governor and professional bureaucrats, who supervised the municipal elections and gave the councillors routine and disagreeable tasks, such as the collection of city taxes. Genuine self-government was not Catherine's intention;

and in any case would have been difficult to implant. For although the official list of towns ran to hundreds, outside St Petersburg and Moscow only three towns could boast even 30,000 inhabitants.

Catherine wished to see the non-Russian provinces more closely knit within the imperial framework. The Provincial Statute was applied, to a greater or lesser degree, in Malorussia, the 'western lands' of the Ukraine annexed from Poland, Siberia, the Crimea and even the Baltic provinces, hitherto virtually autonomous. Use of the Russian language for official business and cultural russification in general, were widely encouraged in the interests of administrative uniformity.

Catherine's provincial reforms—her *'legislomania'*, as she called it—represent a serious attempt to tackle the problem of extending central control throughout the Empire. Her solution, which formed the basis of provincial government for the next eighty years, reflects her lucid and systematic approach. On the other hand, the complex administrative apparatus with its enormous staff was a heavy drain on the treasury. Nor were the personnel as impressive as the institutions. Old habits lingered on; and Catherine's boast, for example, that executive and judiciary were really separate at last, was, as an observer remarked, 'throwing dust in the eyes of Europe'. At bottom, too, the reforms were far less bold and 'liberal' than they seemed. Beneath a façade of enlightened paternalism and decentralization, they were decidedly authoritarian and repressive, with the Pugachov upheaval very much in mind. Catherine's foremost aim was to keep the peasantry under closer control; and new Viceroy was but old *voevoda* writ large.

Finance and the Economy

State expenditure under Catherine tripled, the combined result of the new machinery of provincial government, incessant court extravagance, almost uninterrupted warfare and an economic policy which verged on insouciance—*'J'ai de l'imperturbabilité'*, boasted Catherine. Politics with her came long before economics. To cut a dash—that was her first concern; as to the cost, she faced a soaring budgetary deficit in the spirit of *après moi le déluge*. Even in peacetime, the armed forces automatically absorbed a third of the national revenue; while in the first Turkish war, between 1769 and 1771 alone, the gap between income and expenditure quadrupled. Casting about for remedies Catherine came up with a variety of new but questionable stratagems. She raised costly loans in

Holland and Italy, leaving the awkward legacy of a national debt, amounting at the time of her death, to forty million roubles. Another doubtful new device was to flood the economy with paper banknotes, or *assignats*. By 1796, there were 150 million paper roubles in circulation, worth only two-thirds of their nominal value, and accelerating an already chronic inflationary spiral. Traditional expedients to which Catherine resorted included higher taxation, which, in view of the nobles' exemption from direct taxes, hit hardest at the peasantry, who could least afford to pay. The poll-tax, which still accounted for a third of all revenues, was quadrupled. The excise on salt and spirits was also raised, the spirits-tax alone yielding a fourfold increase. Taxes from trade were another promising source of revenue, with an expanding overseas market and a series of protective tariffs. Industrial revenues also increased fivefold in the last quarter of the century.

Catherine's first priority remained the maintenance and supply of the armed forces, more than ever vital in view of her energetic foreign policy. The army and navy remained completely self-supporting, expertly catered for by fifteen artillery works, three light armament plants and sixty supply factories, producing an annual output of several hundred heavy guns and ammunition and 30,000 muskets. The quality of weapons remained high.

The iron industry in general, however, failed to maintain the lead achieved under Elisabeth, and began to fall behind. Nature here was as much to blame as inferior technology. The ironworks of Karelia and Tula declined, with the exhaustion of their ore and timber resources; and although the Ural foundries continued to operate at full blast, the absence of suitable coal deposits made it impossible for Russia to adopt the new coke-smelting techniques which were revolutionizing iron-production in the west. In addition, the high costs of water transport from the Urals to the Baltic—the journey was commonly staggered over a two-year period—made Russian iron less competitive in western markets.

By contrast, light industry made striking advances, particularly in the Moscow area, where whole village communities were employed in the processing of cloth—flax, hemp, linen, cotton, woollens and silk. In these poorer agricultural regions, it was common for serfs to pay the quitrent partly through the profits of cottage-industries run on a household or a collective basis, on or off the estate. In Moscow *guberniya* in the 1760s, two-thirds of the peasants engaged in part-time work of this

G

kind in addition to agriculture. An important managerial role was played by merchants, and sometimes even peasants. Over half the cloth works were in merchant hands, while one of the leading textile-centres, the village of Ivanovo in Vladimir *guberniya*, with 200 linen workshops, was organized under peasant direction, several of the overseers amassing a considerable capital.

Moreover, the cloth industry was partly run on a wage basis, with hired manpower rather than compulsory labour. For the merchants or peasants who organized the workshops, hired labour proved both cheaper and more efficient than the purchase of serfs at prohibitive prices; this was in any case made increasingly difficult by the tightening noble monopoly of serf ownership. In several merchant enterprises, silk, leather goods, luxury wares and chemical products—hired labour predominated. In the cotton industry, ninety percent of the work force was hired. Several factories were organized along mass-production lines: by 1800, out of 158 linen and woollen factories, six employed over a thousand workers. On the other hand, by far the biggest consumer demand came from the armed forces. As far as aristocratic consumers were concerned, the quality of Russian cloth could not compare with that of western fabrics, which continued to be imported in large quantities. With the gaining of access to the Black Sea, there began on a small scale the export of grain from the southern provinces —the nineteenth-century 'granary of Europe'. As yet, however, passage through the Straits was restricted by Turkey, and the main emporium of trade remained the Baltic, with sixty percent of all overseas trade passing through St Petersburg. Russia continued to maintain a favourable trade-balance, though the gap was narrowed by heavy and rising imports of luxury goods—sugar, coffee, wines, fruit and fabrics, and of raw silks and cottons for processing. While Britain remained Russia's leading customer, there was substantial trade with Denmark, Holland, France and Portugal.

Some historians, attempting to play down Russia's economic backwardness, argue that by 1800 she was easily holding her own with the west. Viewed quantitatively, in terms of productivity and exports, Russia was indeed one of the leading economic powers of the late eighteenth century, with her hundreds of large industrial plants and thousands of smaller workshops, her bargeloads of pig-iron and her bustling docks. On the other hand, however, she possessed few of the basic ingredients which were already revolutionizing the economies of the west. Her economy was still overwhelmingly agrarian. Her urban population was only four percent of the whole, as opposed to seven percent in France and twenty percent in England. The bulk of her wealth lay in the land; only part of her commercial capital was channelled into industry. Industry itself remained an artificial creation of the mercantilist state. It was an arm of its foreign policy, specifically designed to meet the needs of the armed forces, and only secondarily to cater for a small class of aristocratic consumers. The state remained the backbone of industry. It was at once the basic investor and the largest single consumer. It backed non-competitive enterprises with capital and loans, and guaranteed profits by bulk purchases and high protective tariffs. Whatever faint signs of an emerging *bourgeoisie* may be discerned in the activities of merchants, town-dwellers and religious dissenters, the overwhelming predominance of serfdom was bound to act as a brake on the development of capitalist relations. In 1800, the total number of industrial workers was less than 200,000, of whom the majority were serfs or forced labourers, particularly in the all-important ironworks. Light industry was predominantly of the cottage-handicraft or small workshop variety.

For all her veneration of Peter I, Catherine did little to emulate his modernization and mobilization of the economy. Perhaps, in the long run, this may be seen as one of her most serious failings. Although she established the Free Economic Society and a Mining Institute at St Petersburg, with a view to keeping abreast of western advances, she had little real understanding of the implications of industrialization. Russian technology lagged behind, despite isolated flashes of genius. Twenty years before James Watt, a Russian engineer named Polzunov devised a 32 horsepower steam-engine. But although this and other inventions were discussed in the Academy of Sciences and brought to the notice of the government, no effort was made to harness them to industrial production. Serfs still appeared infinitely more profitable than steam-power. Again, though Catherine assigned five percent of her budget to improving communications, she failed to ensure the upkeep of the all-important canal-system which had fallen into neglect since 1725. Finally, Russia failed to develop a mercantile exporter-class. Her overseas commerce remained largely in the hands of English traders at St Petersburg, and the bulk of her goods sailed in British ships.

In the European market, Russia remained a supplier of raw materials and a limited consumer of manufactured goods, rather than an emerging industrial power in her own right. The agrarian character of her economy became more, not less, preponderant as the reign continued. By 1800, iron accounted for only five percent of her exports, as against thirty percent under Elisabeth. The bulk of her exports still consisted of traditional Muscovite wares—timber, flax, hemp, pitch and tallow. Flax and canvas, still in heavy demand by the British admiralty, made up two-fifths of all her exports.

10

Action Abroad

Catherine's most dazzling triumphs were in foreign policy. Though as Grand Duchess she had paraded pacifist views, once in power, she threw herself enthusiastically into a programme of unabashed expansionism. 'I wish to do the governing myself, and to let Europe know it,' she informed Potyomkin. Even by the standards of the age, she was unusually ambitious in her pursuit of grandeur, and boasted that she would risk everything for glory. Although her drive to the Black Sea certainly opened up important economic prospects, her motives at the time were first and foremost political, and her wars were wars of prestige and Great Power status. 'He who gains nothing, loses,' was her maxim, and what she could not gain for herself through diplomatic bluff and brinkmanship, her generals should win for her. 'I have the best army in the world, and money too,' she declared. Once hostilities began, her order was a daredevil 'Hold fast! And not a step backwards!' Not surprisingly, her wars were among the bloodiest and most costly, as well as the most successful, in Russian history, though she contrived to present them to her western admirers as crusades for tolerance and civilization.

Intervention in Poland 1762–1768

The Austrian alliance, pivot of foreign policy since 1726, was dropped. Catherine saw better prospects in joining the late enemy, Prussia, against their vulnerable common neighbour, Poland. Poland, plunged in her habitual anarchy and prostrate from devastation by Russia and Prussia in the Seven Years' War, showed signs of succumbing to pressure from France and Austria. Catherine retaliated by confirming agreements reached between Peter III and Frederick II over the future of Poland, and concluding a formal Russo-Prussian Alliance in 1764.

At the same time, she made sure of Courland (which Poland hoped to annex) by bringing it firmly under Russian control as a satellite-state, nominally ruled by the aged Bühren, now released and reinstated after twenty years in exile.

In 1763, the Polish throne falling vacant, Catherine and Frederick, by a combination of bribes and threats, engineered the election of one of Catherine's former Favourites, Stanislas Pontiatowski. Next, Catherine insinuated herself into the heart of Polish politics by her disingenuous support of the Dissidents, the oppressed non-Catholic (mainly Orthodox) minorities. For Catherine to affect concern for the Dissidents and to demand for them civic rights which she denied her own subjects was, of course, the merest hypocrisy. Her real aim was simply to foster a pro-Russian faction whose grievances she could exploit with a view to further interference. Plans for genuine reform in Poland she automatically vetoed: instead, having exacted concessions for the Dissidents, she forced the Diet to sign a 'treaty of friendship' whereby Russia became the permanent guarantor of the existing Polish constitution. Catherine's design was both to perpetuate Poland's weakness and to legitimize her own right to intervene at will (1768). Yet so brazen was her meddling that no sooner was the treaty signed than a traditionalist Catholic Confederation rose up at Bar to oppose it. When Catherine ordered in her troops to suppress the Confederates, the whole country flared up in civil war.

War with Turkey and Partition of Poland 1768–1772

Turkey, who had long viewed these events with alarm, was not prepared to see Poland trampled down. When Russian irregulars, hunting down the Confederates, crossed into Turkish Moldavia, the Porte declared war, prompted by France and Austria. There followed a long, hard, costly struggle fought on three separate fronts: in Poland (where Russia was embroiled with the Confederates), on the Lower Danube, and in the Crimea. Almost at once, Moldavia-Wallachia fell under Russian occupation with the victories of Larga and Kagul (1770).

Meanwhile, a unique drama unfolded itself at sea, when Catherine's Baltic fleet made its circuitous voyage via the North Sea and the Bay of Biscay to beard the Turks in the Levant. In a sensational victory off Cape Chesme in Asia Minor, the Turkish fleet was annihilated (1770). Such a triumph was close to Catherine's heart, attracting as it did the awed attention of the Powers. But like her land victories, it was not followed up with sufficient drive; 1771 saw the Crimea overrun, but ended inconclusively.

Meanwhile, Russian advances in the Balkans were arousing concern at Vienna. Austria was not prepared to see Russia permanently installed on the Danube, a traditional Habsburg preserve, and made ready to join Turkey in dislodging her. Frederick II, alarmed at the imminent prospect of an Austro-Russian war in which he would be involved as Catherine's ally, suggested that Austria and Russia compose their differences by assuaging their territorial appetites at the expense of Poland. Hitherto, Catherine had rejected the idea of partitioning Poland as contrary to Russia's best interests; but now, beset by internal unrest as well as by the Austrian threat, she agreed to drop her claims for Danubian spoils in return for compensation in Poland. In 1772, on the pretext of restoring order, Russia, Austria and Prussia stripped Poland of a third of her territory and population. To Russia went the former 'western lands' up to the Dvina—most of Polish Livonia, Polotsk, Vitebsk and Mstislavl. Once begun, the process of partition proved hard to stop, and Poland was inexorably to be swallowed up, province by province, by her avaricious neighbours.

Expansionism Triumphant 1772–1792

In 1772, negotiations between Russia and Turkey opened at Fokshany. Catherine, though prepared to evacuate the Balkans, insisted that the Crimea be detached from its dependence on Turkey. Turkey's refusal led to renewed hostilities. Once more, Russian victories forced the Turks back to the conference table; while for Catherine the Pugachov rebellion made peace imperative. In 1774 was concluded the Treaty of Kuchuk-Kainardzhi, which ranks with that of Nystadt as a milestone in Russian history. With the acquisition of the entire coastline between the Bug, Dnieper, the Sea of Azov and Kabardia, Russia at last gained access to the Black Sea. No longer a Turkish lake, 'a pure and immaculate virgin', it now lay open to Russian ships, affording access to the west via the Aegean and Mediterranean. In addition, the Crimea became formally independent; and with Russian bases at Kerch and Yenikale, inevitably fell under Russian influence. Finally, Russia was declared official protector of the Christian minorities in the Ottoman Empire, with special interests in Moldavia-Wallachia. The humiliations of 1711 and 1739 were amply avenged by this overwhelming triumph. For Catherine, the occasion was 'one of the happiest in my life'.

Yet massive as her victory was, she had still grander schemes in mind. Her replacement of the cautious Panin by the bold and dynamic Potyomkin on the Imperial Council signified the adoption of a still more militant expansionism. This envisaged Turkey's final expulsion from Europe and the partition of her European possessions; the restoration of a 'Greek Empire' to be ruled from Constantinople by Catherine's second grandson, Constantine; and the creation of a satellite-state in Moldavia-Wallachia and Bessarabia. The Prussian alliance, having served its purpose, was abandoned and agreement to partition the Balkans was reached with Austria (1782). In 1783, a pro-Russian revolt was fomented in the Crimea. Russian troops were poured in, and 'the pimple on Russia's nose', as Potyomkin called the Crimea, was formally annexed. Friction with Turkey was deliberately inflamed. In 1787, Catherine, Joseph II, and an entourage of western ambassadors went on a well-publicized tour of the south, including a visit to the new naval base at Sebastopol. Within months, the Porte declared war.

Catherine's second Turkish War was, however, no easy feat. An Austro-Russian thrust into Moldavia-Wallachia encountered strong resistance. The key fortress of Ochakov, besieged by Potyomkin, held out through the whole of 1788, until falling to a final epic assault with enormous loss of life. Moreover, Catherine was faced with the hostility of Britain and France, determined to resist any further upset to the balance of power in the Levant. Sweden launched a surprise-attack from the north in 1788; the gunfire of Swedish battleships was heard at St Petersburg. Poland, too, was once more up in arms. Forces had to be diverted to deal with these secondary threats. But meanwhile, the Balkan campaign of 1789 brought greater success with Suvorov's signal victory at Rymnik; and the advancing Austrians took Belgrade and Bucharest. All seemed set for victory, when the sudden death of Joseph II removed Austria from the war. Russia was left to deal Turkey the final blow alone. In 1790, Suvorov took the fortress of Izmail at the mouth of the Danube, while the Russian fleet dealt a series of devastating blows to the Turkish flotillas.

At the Peace of Jassy (1792), the Treaty of Kuchuk-Kainardzhi was confirmed together with Russian sovereignty over the Crimea. In addition, Russia's south-west frontier was extended to the Dniester, at the mouth of which was founded the city of Odessa. Though this fell somewhat short of her original hopes. Catherine could survey the overall result of her Turkish wars with some complacency. The Black Sea littoral from the Dniester to the Kuban was hers. The fertile southern steppes of the Ukraine, long a prey to the Crimean Tartars, were safe for colonization. The Crimea developed rapidly with the foundation of Sebastopol, Yekaterinoslav, Kherson and Nikolaev.

Poland—The Final Partitions

Russia's imbroglio with Turkey seemed Poland's cue for action. The Poles signed an ill-fated alliance with Prussia and introduced a series of constitutional reforms aimed at making Poland strong and independent (1791). For that very reason, Catherine was resolved to scotch them. This time she evoked the spectre of the French Revolution, which she claimed to see as the centre of an international conspiracy aimed at subverting monarchy across Europe. Encouraging Prussia and Austria to intervene in France, she undertook to smash 'jacobinism' in Poland.

Her hands once free in the south, she ordered her armies into Poland. Once again, she was welcomed by a Polish faction which invited her to put down the reformers. When the latter called on Prussia to honour her alliance, the Prussians not only reneged absolutely, but baulked of victories in France, joined eagerly with Russia in dismembering Poland. By the second partition of 1793, Russia annexed the provinces of Vilna, Minsk, Kiev, Volhynia and Podolia, and took control of the rump Poland which remained.

The end came swiftly. When the Poles rose up under Kosciuszko in a last desperate bid for independence, Russia and Prussia at once intervened again. After Kosciuszko's capture and Suvorov's storming of Warsaw the revolt quickly collapsed. In the third and final partition (1795) Russia formally annexed Courland and absorbed the rest of Livonia. Poland was now no more than a geographical expression: the Great Power of the seventeenth century had been wiped off the map. Though Catherine's policy was acclaimed with rapture at St Petersburg, a few rightly doubted its wisdom. In the first place, partition had come about not from deliberate policy, but as a result of Catherine's irresponsible opportunism. For the sake of immediate and easy gain, Catherine had deprived Russia of a useful buffer-state protecting her from her neighbours: both Prussia and Austria now bordered Russia directly. Further, Russia was now permanently tied to this 'robbers' alliance', and lost much of her freedom of action. It is true that the territories annexed by Catherine were mainly Orthodox and Belorussian in population and had belonged to Russia in the Middle Ages. It is questionable, however, whether Russian interests were really served by allowing Prussia and Austria to share an influence in Poland which Russia had hitherto enjoyed alone.

Catherine's territorial gains were Russia's greatest since Ivan IV. Of Russia's fifty provinces, eleven consisted of new acquisitions. These successes rested as ever on a large, effective and powerful army, numbering half a million men by the close of the reign, seconded by a warfleet of 70 battleships and 40 frigates. Russia's international role was significantly heightened. If, in 1762, she was one of the leading European Powers, by 1796 she was arguably first among equals. Undefeated and seemingly invincible, Catherine played an increasingly prominent part in Europe's affairs. 'In our time,' recalled one of her foreign ministers, 'not a cannon dared fire in Europe without our consent.' Her victories over Turkey and Poland demolished France's traditional 'eastern barrier'. She defied Britain by sponsoring the League of Armed Neutrality against her (1780). By her mediation in the War of the Bavarian Succession (1779), she became protector of the Imperial constitution, with a voice in German affairs, a commitment strengthened by close family ties with German royalty. On the eve of her death, appalled by events in France and the menace of the Revolution, she prepared to embark on direct military intervention in defence of the *ancien régime*.

11

The 'Golden Age' of the Nobility

Nobility and Service

The *Manifesto* of 1762 reflects a growing sense of personal honour and class-solidarity among the nobility. No longer was the noble a nameless cog in the wheels of state, obliged by law to perform service; but a volunteer, requested by the state to assist it by virtue of his superior education and skills. Such sentiments found expression in demands voiced at the Legislative Commission for preferential social treatment. What was desired was a formal guarantee of rights, including security of property and greater local powers. Specifically, the noble wanted pledges of his exclusive and inalienable tenure of land and serfs, and immunity from the arbitrary arrests, banishments and confiscations so commonplace in the age of palace-revolutions.

In theory, the nobles' aspirations were granted by Catherine in the Charter of the Nobility (1785) which formally pronounced the nobility to be a privileged estate of the realm. Their rights granted over the previous sixty years were confirmed and extended. Their security of person and property were guaranteed. They continued to enjoy a monopoly of land and serf ownership, to which was added control of the natural resources on their land. They were free to set up industrial enterprises on their estates and market their products at home or abroad. They could not be punished without trial, and could be tried only by their peers. They were exempt from compulsory service, taxation, and now too from corporal punishment and the billeting of troops on their land. They were authorized to hold corporate Assemblies of the Nobility in each province every three years, and to petition the Governor concerning their needs. To placate devotees of aristocracy, like

Shcherbatov, the pedigree of each noble was to be recorded in a special genealogical roster, a kind of Burke's peerage, under six separate categories, of which the sixth and most illustrious was reserved for those whose blue blood could be traced back to Muscovite times or earlier.

But though ostensibly the nobles might seem to have acquired the standing of a genuine aristocracy, in fact they were still very much at the state's disposal. The notion of the Charter as a Russian Magna Carta, marking the political emancipation of the nobility, is quite erroneous. There was no question of the nobility blocking or offsetting the power of the state. On the contrary, autocratic power in the provinces was firmly vested in the Governor, as the Empress's plenipotentiary. Furthermore, the Charter specifically reminded the noble of his duty to engage immediately in the service should the autocrat so command. The monarch's disapproval of those who evaded service showed itself in her refusal to receive them at court, the supreme social failure. The chief purpose of the Assemblies, in any case, was administrative— to facilitate the election of local officials. Moreover, not only was a noble without a service-record ineligible for elective office, but all elected officials were strictly subordinate to the Governor, and liable at any time to dismissal.

In any case, as the reign of Paul was to show, Charter or no Charter, nobles were no more immune than before to arbitrary deprivation of their freedom or property, not to mention corporal punishment, at the quirks of the autocrat, without any means of redress, and without the least vestige of corporate resistance or protest from their peers. Paul's notorious remark—that the only distinguished person in Russia was he whom the monarch condescended to address, and at that only for as long as he spoke to him—whether authentic or apocryphal, trenchantly sums up the true position of the noble.

The nobles were also dependent on the state in a more basic sense. By the 1760s they were reckoned to number with their families half a million persons. The splintering of estates by equal inheritance could beggar a noble family within three generations. Even the greatest landowners lived in the shadow of bankruptcy. Nikolai Sheremetev, who owned more serfs than any landowner in Russia, was in debt to the tune of two million roubles. Struggling to keep pace with the rising costs of westernized living, the nobles grew increasingly indebted to the state. Many relied on the state to provide educational grants. In one province, two hundred young men complained to the marshal of the nobility of being unable to enter the service for lack of suitable clothing and footwear. In 1786 was founded a State Loan Bank, with a capital of eleven million roubles (as opposed to the three-quarters of a million at the disposal of the archetypal Bank of the Nobility in 1754). By 1800, the state was disbursing more in loans to noblemen than it spent in any other single area. Conversely, within forty years of Catherine's death, two-thirds of all landed estates were mortgaged to the government.

The new-found sense of honour, then, should not be misconstrued. Official rank still had the edge on noble birth, as western visitors noted with astonishment. 'A gentleman counts for nothing here,' observed one Englishman; while the British ambassador explained that 'all nobles are equal, and have precedence only according to the rank of their employment in the state.' True, Catherine paid token respect to blue blood; but this was out of political convenience. It tickled her vanity to make much of the ancient families, and it suited her purpose to increase their dependence on her with generous financial grants. If she filled her court with aristocrats, and sent Golitsyns, Dolgorukys and other blue-blooded nobles to represent her abroad, it was because she appreciated the prestige value of such gestures. Whatever social pre-eminence she might accord to blue blood, she retained a tight grip on political power. Shcherbatov might still argue for a caste-system based on birth. But his was a minority view. The nobility as a whole echoed the sentiments of the memoirist who wrote that 'State-service in Russia is life', and compared retirement to a living death. It was not pedigree, but length of service that constituted the chief source of family pride.

Military rank was especially sought after: hence the popularity of Catherine's wars, which offered prospects of rapid promotion. There arose a growing sense of national consciousness and patriotic pride in service, a genuine spirit of self-sacrifice and heroism, which was to emerge on an epic scale in the 'Patriotic War' of 1812. Under Catherine, there was an added undertone of gallantry and chivalry in serving the Empress, an element which she consciously fostered with her character-istic graciousness. The mystique of rank was symbolized in membership of the honorary orders of St Vladimir, St Andrew and St Anne, instituted by Peter I, each with its appropriate star, ribbon and cere-monial. As with his Junker counterpart, the noble's proudest boast was his military feats. Typical of the noble pride were the parting words of a father to a young noble leaving home to take up his commission: 'I had rather hear of your death, than that you disgraced yourself.' More than just the title of an opera, *A Life for the Czar* came to symbolize a philosophy of life. The noble's ethos, then, still derived first and foremost from the state: his sense of solidarity was with his fellow students at the Cadet Corps or his messmates in the Guards, rather than with the provincial Assembly.

The bureaucratic apparatus expanded enormously after the provincial reforms of 1775; and here, although the top administrative posts were usually held by hereditary nobles, the lower and middle echelons saw a significant influx of personnel of non-noble origin. This exacerbated the traditional rivalry between the military and civil branches: while the military looked down on the 'penpushers', the bureaucrats strove to ape the military. The noble ethos, transferred from the military to the civilian sphere, tended to show its less attractive side: blind obedience to orders, without regard to considerations of consistency or even humanity; a blend of obsequious servility towards higher authorities, and curtness and arbitrariness towards inferiors and civilians. Such attitudes, the favourite targets of nineteenth-century social satire, were part of everyday life under Catherine. So too, were bribery and extortion. It was common knowledge that no piece of official business, no lawsuit could be properly expedited without a fee on the side; and peculation was rife. As a rule, the state connived at this; it was, after all, one means of supplementing inadequate salaries. Only if it reached scandalous proportions did Catherine feel obliged to register token disapproval: to one Governor-General she sent a large empty purse as a hint that his extortions had not gone unnoticed. For all this corruption, however, it may be supposed that the bureaucracy included as many intelligent, conscientious and honest civil servants, as not. At any rate, official positions were rarely for sale; they were always retained and allocated by the state; and although ranks were occasionally sold, they never became perquisites of noble families, as in France.

Serfdom

Provincial life was an increasingly important source of the nobleman's income. Rising living-costs and chronic inflation made a more effective exploitation of serf-labour a pressing necessity, since serf-ownership brought minimal profits rather than affluence. Frugality and parsimony were the general rule in estate-management. In all but imported luxury goods, estates were usually self-supporting. Raw materials produced on the estates were processed on the spot by serf carpenters, smiths, cobblers and distillers. Farming methods remained as rudimentary as ever and there was little knowledge of the new fodder-crops that were revolutionizing western agriculture. A successful harvest was still largely a matter of chance, and the soil was quickly becoming exhausted. Only the Ukraine and the newly annexed southern provinces regularly yielded good harvests. In the central and northern provinces, serfs were tied to overworked and unproductive land. This was to create a legacy of rural impoverishment and overpopulation.

In 1765, Catherine founded the Free Economic Society, one aim of which was to promote the study of western advances in agriculture and the adoption of improved methods of estate-management. The majority of nobles, however, preoccupied with their service-careers, had little inclination for study. They continued to leave relatives and bailiffs in charge of their estates, to run them as best they could. In their view, whatever advantages might eventually derive from western models, the most effective means of increasing profits was still to sqeeze them out of the peasants. Even the more advanced members of the Free Economic Society tended to regard the Enlightenment less as a spur to humanitarian reform, than as a rationale for the more efficient exploitation of serf labour. The reign witnessed a marked extension and re-intensification of the *corvée* and quitrent systems across the Empire. The average quitrent doubled. The *corvée* was introduced on a large scale in the east and south-east. Frequently, it exceeded three days a week, and work on Sundays and Church holidays was far from rare.

Catherine began by finding serfdom an inhuman anachronism; she ended by accepting it as an inescapable fact of life. In the first years of her reign, she had hopes of at least mitigating its worst aspects through government control of serf-noble relations (as in Austria and Prussia), and by making over plots of land into peasant-ownership. To test her views on her advisers and on the nobility in general, Catherine launched several *balons d'essai*. The Free Economic Society was one. Catherine hoped that a realization of the economic advantages of a free labour force might induce the nobility to consider the reduction of serfdom out of self-interest, if not out of humanity.

Among the first undertakings of the Free Economic Society was an international essay-competition (set and judged by Catherine) on the desirability of peasant proprietorship. The winning entry, submitted by a French *savant*, recommended that peasants be granted small plots of land. In the first drafts of the *Nakaz*, Catherine proposed state regulation of serf conditions, suggesting that *corvée* and quitrent should be limited and equitable, that serfs be permitted to buy their freedom, and be protected by law against abuse. Even in the published text of the *Nakaz*, she hinted unequivocally at the need for reform and her desire to see a property-owning peasantry. The Legislative Commission, however quickly showed that her views were too advanced for the nobility. If her personal advisers, Panin and Vyazemsky, shook their heads over her ideas, the outspoken Shcherbatov voiced the feelings of the nobility in general. Shcherbatov resented the very presence of the serf question in the Commission's agenda and feared the effect of rumours at a time of mounting peasant unrest.

If Catherine failed to elicit sympathy from the educated and western-ized Shcherbatov, how could she hope to win over the provincial squires, the overwhelming bulk of the nobility? On such a controversial issue she could only force matters at risk of endangering her own position. Indeed, from the outset of her reign, she was obliged to set the record straight. Within a month of her accession she declared her determination 'vigorously to protect the noble landowners in their land and goods'.

In effect, then, having tested public opinion and finding it hostile to reform, Catherine abandoned her original hopes as unrealistic, and indeed, dangerous to herself.

The serfs' plight, already desperate, deteriorated from year to year. Serfdom was a lifelong and hereditary condition. The serf was tied permanently to his master's estate: without written permission he could go neither from one estate to another nor from one village to another on the same estate. He was as much a piece of the noble's property as the landlord's cattle or horses. In law, he was simply a moveable chattel: the noble could buy and sell him, give him away as a present or a bribe, in payment of debts or as a wager at cards. He could dispose of him as he thought fit, singly or with his family, with land or without; he could uproot a household or a whole village. Serfs were put up for auction (often in the same lots as cattle) and were advertised in newspapers. In the *St Petersburg News*, entries such as these appeared regularly: 'Sixteen-year old peasant-girl for sale; well-behaved; price twenty roubles'; 'Good musician for sale; excellent conductor; price eight hundred roubles'; or 'For sale: one wigmaker and a cow of good stock'.

The noble assumed the right to force serfs into marriage. No serf could wed without his master's permission, and compulsory marriages were common, dictated purely by economic concern regardless of the feelings of the pair concerned. A correspondent of the Free Economic Society observed virtuously in 1791: 'Good farmers try to breed cattle and poultry, and the civilized man should care even more, with the help of God, for the breeding of human stock'. Some nobles levied fines on the families of peasant girls who remained unwed after the age of twenty, and ordered widows to remarry.

The juridical and penal rights of noble over serf were unlimited. The government made no attempt to regulate the penalties which the noble might choose to inflict, beyond a token prohibition of the death penalty. Some nobles drew up their own printed regulations and punishments. Already, Elisabeth had invited nobles to send serfs to Siberia in return for financial compensation. Under Catherine this privilege was flagrantly abused: peasants guilty of no more than old-age and incapacity were sent off on the long trek eastwards, in order that their master might reap the compensation while keeping the young and able-bodied on the estate. In 1765, the noble was empowered to mete out sentences of hard labour for any length of time, and in 1767 serfs were formally forbidden to appeal to the authorities against their masters. Any such complaint was automatically classed as a false and malicious report, for which the punishment was public knouting and exile for life.

The noble could call on the police or local militia to suppress disturbances. Procedure in such cases was laid down in special regulations. First, the local clergy were to exhort the recalcitrant serfs to submit. If this failed, the peasant grain stocks were to be set on fire. Next, the troops were to intimidate the serfs by shooting above their heads. Finally, they were to open fire on them. Sometimes even artillery was brought in.

Household serfs were especially liable to abuse. Notorious was the case of the female landowner, Dar'ya Saltykova, who was found to have tortured to death over a hundred serfs for the most trifling peccadillos. Even a moderately enlightened noble had his offending serfs stripped, tarred with pitch and led through the village as an example. Such serfs were often further humiliated by having half their head shaved. Of course, not all nobles were brutes and sadists. There were many who strove to govern justly and paternally. The father of the writer Radishchev was liked and respected by his serfs, who hid and

H

protected him during the Pugachov rebellion. But the institution of serfdom as it existed under Catherine lay wide open to abuse. On the other hand, barely half a dozen cases of abuse were officially brought to light during the reign; and offenders were let off with derisory sentences.

The number of serfs in the Empire all but doubled under Catherine. This was mainly the result of territorial expansion, serfdom being immediately introduced in the conquered areas. But the problem was also aggravated by Catherine's own lavish distributions. Peter I, Anna and Elisabeth had all been generous in rewarding their supporters, but Catherine far surpassed them by transferring nearly a million serfs into private hands. In one day alone in 1762, she gave away 16,000 serfs, and again in 1795 she disposed of 100,000 at one stroke. Ex-Favourites and superannuated statesmen received enormous numbers. Such generosity was an indispensable part of Catherine's political system, her bounties taking the edge off disgruntlement and preventing the formation of opposition cliques.

Catherine's wars took a fearful toll of peasant lives. In 1773, the army quota of recruits rose from one peasant per 150 to one per 100. Casualties for the reign are put as high as half a million. For those killed in battle, many perished of disease on the unhealthy Black Sea littoral and Lower Danube region, where Potyomkin himself succumbed. Service was still for twenty-five years, and discipline, still based on the Military Statute of 1716, remained notoriously harsh. New recruits were often marched into camp under guard and lodged in gaols to prevent desertion.

The Pugachov Rebellion

Peasant discontent, which had been brimming up under Elisabeth, erupted with alarming frequency under Catherine. To add to the chronic general unrest, it was widely rumoured among the people that Peter III had been on the point of decreeing peasant emancipation at the time of his mysterious demise. Garbled and exaggerated accounts of the debates on serfdom at the Legislative Commission, filtered down across the country, arousing much wishful thinking. These rising hopes were rudely dashed by the reintensification of serfdom and the rise in taxes; and popular frustration found vent in mounting violence. In Moscow *guberniya*, between 1764 and 1769 alone, some thirty landowners were slain by their serfs. In 1770 rebellion flared up in Karelia. In 1771, with an outbreak of plague at Moscow, rioting mobs terrorized the city for three days, and murdered the archbishop. Pretenders reappeared in several regions, raising a banner of legitimacy behind which the peasant could rally with a clear conscience. Some two dozen self-styled 'Peter IIIs' sprang up in the course of the reign.

It was under the leadership of one such Pretender, the Don Cossack Emel'yan Pugachov, that there erupted the most momentous peasant rebellion in czarist Russia. Pugachov, a former deserter from Catherine's armies, was a shrewd and resourceful adventurer, with the ability to articulate pent-up popular grievances and to fuse the aspirations of essentially disparate groups into a united movement. His message was attractively simple and couched in the terminology of popular lore. He, Pugachov, was the rightful Czar Peter III, come to restore justice to his downtrodden subjects. He undertook to free them, not, indeed, from service to the 'Czar', which formed an integral part of the peasant cosmology, but from alien ways and cruel bondage—the *corvée*, quit-rent, forced labour and religious oppression—forced upon them by treacherous taskmasters who had come between the 'Czar' and his people. For them, nobles and officials of every sort, Pugachov's mani-festoes were grimly explicit—'Seize them, punish them, hang them: do to them as they, having no Christian feeling, oppressed you.'

The rebellion ignited in 1773 among the mixed populations of the Ural river around Orenburg, a remote frontier region and thinly garrisoned outpost of empire, where unrest took on a national character. Non-Russian nomadic peoples, Kirghiz, Kalmyks, Bashkirs and Cossacks, each labouring under a variety of grievances, were eager, for different reasons, to rise up against the colonial oppressor in their midst. After unsuccessfully laying siege to Orenburg, Pugachov wintered in the Urals. Here, the ranks of his followers were swelled by industrial serfs, fleeing *en masse* from the factories and mines, where conditions were unusually burdensome, even women and children being forced into slave labour. The Old Believers—who included most of the Cos-sacks—lately subject to intense proselytization, flocked to Pugachov's side, attracted by his pledge of religious freedom. The whole of south-east Russia—where the recent imposition of the *corvée* sparked off bitter resentment—flared up in violence.

When government detachments were wiped out by the rebels, the movement began to assume grave proportions. In 1774, Pugachov

advanced slowly to the Volga, with a large and motley array of
followers, supplies and even artillery, to lay siege to Kazan. Panic seized
the nobility, as dire rumours reached Moscow and St Petersburg. In the
central provinces, anticipating Pugachov's arrival, serfs rose up spon-
taneously in their tens of thousands. Provincial government collapsed,
as outnumbered troops defected, and terrified officials abandoned their
posts. Towns opened their gates to receive the rebels. Nobles who fell
into their hands were strung up on gallows, or massacred by their serfs,
who spared neither age nor sex. Country mansions were sacked and
gutted, the hated appurtenances of western life torn down and destroyed. Breaking into warehouses, the peasants took their fill of salt and
spirits, free from the need to pay the hated excise.

After the fall of Kazan, Catherine, who had tried to dismiss the revolt
as a 'vile comedy', took resolute counter-measures, placing the stern
and efficient general Panin★ in charge of operations, and hastily recalling
divisions from the Turkish front. This was a tacit admission that what
she had on her hands was little less than outright civil war. Pugachov
unexpectedly broke off his successful advance, but his nominal with-
drawal southwards along the west bank of the Volga, via Penza and
Saratov, resembled a triumphal progress, as rebellion fanned out across
the countryside with undiminished virulence. But with regular troops
in well co-ordinated and relentless pursuit, the break-up of his hetero-
geneous *jacquerie* was only a matter of time. At length, his ever-
dwindling forces were smashed near Tsaritsyn. Betrayed by his remain-
ing Cossack followers, Pugachov was surrendered to Panin, and placed
like a wild beast, in an iron cage.

The rebellion once subdued, the government forces switched to
mopping-up operations of hideous severity. Panin gave the word for
an official vendetta, a class-war in reverse, in which the nobility,
still heady with shock, settled its scores with bloodthirsty vindictive-
ness. Troops poured into the recent trouble-spots, and in their train
officials of the Secret Chancery. Summary courts-martial meted out
mass reprisals. Gallows, wheels and gibbets lined the roadsides and
village squares, or were floated down the Volga on rafts, exhibiting the
gruesome corpses of the convicted. To this policy of deliberate terror
Catherine gave her reluctant consent 'for the good of the Empire'.
Pugachov himself, still in his iron cage, was conveyed to Moscow for
interrogation by Sheshkovsky, who, as Catherine delicately observed,

★ Brother of the Foreign Minister.

'has a way with the common people'. He was speedily tried and publicly beheaded. Though Panin and the *Generalitet* grumbled that the spectacle would have been more effective had he had first been quartered alive, it was still, as an eyewitness remarked, 'the true triumph of the gentry'.

The significance of the rebellion lies less in its scale, remarkable as it was, than in its psychological impact. Alarming and sanguinary while it lasted—indeed, it was Europe's greatest social upheaval before the French Revolution—it is unlikely that the rebellion ever stood a real chance of succeeding. The fears and hatreds which it aroused, on the other hand, produced deep, lasting and fateful effects on the outlook of nobility and government. Relief at danger overcome and outrage that unrest could have been allowed to get out of hand, led to an uncompromising determination to forestall any possible recurrence by the imposition of far tighter controls. The rebellion served to divide society more rigidly than ever into 'two nations'. At best, the peasant was regarded as a wayward and unruly child; at worst, as a mutinous savage. Either way, the moral was the same: he was to be kept firmly in his place. Reformist views took on an untimely and even subversive aspect, especially in the light of events in France.

Although all subsequent peasant outbreaks under Catherine were local and sporadic in character (over 250 separate incidents are recorded in the central *gubernii* alone, with a sharp rise at the time of the French Revolution) they were thought serious enough to warrant a correspondingly steep increase in the volume of troops quartered in the provinces. By 1796, order in the countryside was being maintained by no less than one-third of the entire army, under a virtual system of martial law. Whatever her original hopes, there was no longer for Catherine any question of enlightened social reform: the *'canaille'*, she agreed, must be held firmly down.

12

The Russian Enlightenment

Education

In the early years of her reign, Catherine had high hopes of education as a short cut to making Russia a truly 'European power'. Her optimism found solid support in the writings of the Encyclopedists and apparent corroboration in the history of Peter I: society, she believed, could be remoulded by informed and high-minded endeavour. Where Peter had used coercion and violence, however, Catherine aspired to succeed through the co-operation of an enlightened elite and an educated public opinion. By removing children from a traditional Russian environment and exposing them to selected civilizing influences, she hoped to create what she called 'a new type of men', who, as future statesmen and leaders of society, would be in a position to put her ideals into practice.

At her instigation, the enlightened humanitarian, Betsky, a devotee of Locke and Rousseau, embarked on a variety of educational experiments. He set up Foundlings' Homes at both capitals, reorganized the Cadet Corps, and provided for female education, hitherto sadly neglected, by the establishment of the Smol'ny Institute at St Petersburg. Eschewing the traditional emphasis on formal instruction, strict discipline and corporal punishment, Betsky stressed the inculcation of 'gentle manners' and the development of the individual. As well as conventional academic and vocational studies, the pupils at the Cadet Corps and Smol'ny Institute were encouraged to take up music, literature and the fine arts, and to develop intellectual discernment and moral awareness. The aim was to produce a rounded and cultivated personality, free from native prejudices and the marks of narrow specialization, and receptive to western ideas. The officer-cadets should be not merely military types, but 'knowledgeable citizens' and 'true sons of the fatherland', capable of informed and responsible attitudes. While Catherine was to be disappointed in her lofty hopes, and indeed shocked by low academic standards—she had the satisfaction of superintending the emergence of a generation of young men and women of the world, with much social grace, poise and *savoir-faire*. For in essence, the Cadet Corps, Smol'ny Institute, and some sixty residential academies and *pensions* modelled on them—were still hardly more than aristocratic finishing-schools. Even so, by bringing up young men together as an intellectual elite, in isolation from outside realities, and imbuing them with modern norms and ideas, such schools did nurture in some pupils a critical and objective attitude towards their country. It was from a similar background of experiences that the Decembrist movement was to germinate. Such an outlook could also result from Catherine's policy of sending promising students on to western universities. The most notable such example was that of the writer Radishchev, whose crucial formative impressions were gained as a student at Leipzig under imperial patronage.

Towards the end of the reign, Catherine turned to more conventional methods and accepted the need for a nationwide system of general education. Impressed by the Austrian system introduced by Joseph II, she called for the adoption of similar facilities in Russia. In 1786, she authorized provincial capitals to set up elementary and secondary schools, open both to nobles and non-nobles. As a solution to the educational needs of the Empire, however, this project fell woefully short. In the first place, Catherine belied her good intentions by her paltry contributions. Only two percent of her budget was allocated to education; and of this, she diverted ten times more to the Smol'ny Institute alone than to all the schools in a single province. Trained teachers were in short supply, were poorly paid and enjoyed little social status. Lastly, despite Catherine's wish to see the schools attended by children of various classes, they were in practice boycotted by the nobility, reluctant to mix with their social inferiors.

No provision was made for serf education. As Catherine confided to an adviser: 'The *canaille* must not be educated to the point where they know as much as you or I, and refuse to obey us'. By her death, only two children out of a thousand received a secondary schooling; and all told there were only 550 educational institutes in Russia, at a time when France boasted 8,000 elementary schools alone. Education for the most part remained the privilege of the ruling class. Popular instruction, such as it was, continued to rely heavily on provincial garrison-schools, parish schools and church seminaries.

Art and Letters

Catherine's vaunted patronage of the arts was a characteristic and integral aspect of her statecraft. She valued them less as a connoisseur than as a propagandist. Her assiduous attendance at chamber-concerts and the Italian opera was not affected by the fact that she was tone-deaf; and it was as much for her own image as that of her capital that she set out to crown her predecessors' work by making St Petersburg the 'Palmyra of the north', one of the most splendid of European courts. 'Great buildings,' as she declared, 'attest no less to the grandeur of a reign than great deeds.' Likewise she amassed at fabulous cost a prodigious collection of old masters, to enhance alike her palaces and her reputation. In keeping with her heroic and pagan tastes (Plutarch was among her favourite authors) the caprices and curlicues of the Elisabethan rococo yielded to a calm and stately classicism. The imperial grounds at Czarskoe Selo, with their rostral columns, triumphal arches and other impressive monuments to her Turkish victories, evoked, as she intended they should, the glories of the ancient world: her reign too should be spoken of in the same breath as that of Alexander the Great or Augustus, just as her patronage of the arts might compare with that of Louis XIV. Her preference for Roman dignity is reflected in the palladian serenity of the Alexander Palace by Quarenghi, and the Cameron Gallery, both at Czarskoe Selo. The Cameron Gallery, approached by a magnificent double flight of steps, provided Catherine with a favourite covered walk, which contrived to be both inspiring and intimate, with its long, graceful Ionic portico, where, between each column, the Empress beheld a bronze bust of her heroes from ancient and modern history. Another of Cameron's creations was the Palace of Pavlovsk, Catherine's gift to her son. To this stately pile, with its echoes of the Pantheon at Rome, and its Pompeian and Grecian interiors, Cameron also supplied a sentimental note in the spacious, rolling grounds, with his fragile and delicate pavilion of the Three Graces and Temple of Friendship, inspired by the Trianon at Versailles.

The Academy of Fine Arts, under Betsky's direction, began to turn out Russian architects and artists of singular distinction. Notable were Bazhonov, who designed one of Moscow's most stately and impressive edifices, the Pashkov Mansion;* and Starov, creator of the magnificent Taurid Palace at St Petersburg, Catherine's gift to Potyomkin. Built to commemorate Potyomkin's Crimean triumphs, the Palace was Greek rather than Roman in inspiration, a superbly harmonious ensemble, with a unique unity and purity of conception which influenced public architecture in Russia well into the next century. Of Russian painters whose work compares with the best of eighteenth-century art, Levitsky excelled both in formal court portraiture, and in more intimate, delicate studies, such as those commissioned by Catherine of the young *pension-naires* at the Smol'ny Institute. One of the undoubted geniuses of the age was the sculptor Shubin, whose radiantly eloquent busts of Catherine, Lomonosov and Potyomkin rank among the gems of Russian classical art. Shubin's marbles seem almost to breathe, such is their outstanding facial expressiveness.

Theatrical and musical life also flourished under court and private patronage. Italian opera continued to be the rage of St Petersburg. By 1800 there were fifteen theatres in Moscow alone. In the countryside, some nobles organized their own serf theatres and orchestras.

Catherine presided over a sweeping upsurge in the spread of knowledge and the cultivation of *belles-lettres*. The Academy of Sciences and Moscow University put out an ever-increasing flow of books and literary journals. In 1769 alone, eight new periodicals appeared. At Catherine's behest, an impressive array of western authors was systematically translated, placing the pick of classical and modern literature at the disposal of the reading public. She actively encouraged private initiative: in 1783, she granted nobles the right to set up their own printing-presses. Despite repression and censorship at the end of the reign, publishing and the book trade began in earnest. Of all books published in eighteenth-century Russia, ninety percent—over 8,500 titles—appeared after 1750.

Catherine also nurtured a developing interest in Russian history and culture. With her approval, Novikov and Shcherbatov published archival documents. Shcherbatov, as imperial historiographer, produced the first scholarly *History of Russia*. The study of language and literature received official sanction with the founding in 1783 of the Russian Academy, which enlisted nearly every Russian writer of note in the compilation of the first *Dictionary* of the Russian language.

The age witnessed a flowering of literature. The predominant style
* Now the Lenin Library.

remained the pseudo-classical, well-suited to themes of national grandeur. Kheraskov produced Russia's first epic poem, the *Rossiada* (1779), in which the theme of liberation from the Tartars subtly mirrors Catherine's Turkish victories. The dramatist Sumarokov, in his national tragedy, *Dimitry the Pretender* (1771), allegorized the solidarity of monarch and nobility and their joint triumph over rebellion. In his heroes, drawn from Russian history and legend, Sumarokov flattered his audiences by portraying the nobility as paragons of honour and high-minded self-sacrifice. By contrast, Fonvizin, in two delightful comedies of manners, *The Brigadier* (1766) and *The Minor* (1782), tellingly poked fun at the provincial gentry for their apish gallomania and dismal cultural standards. In *The Minor*, Fonvizin created two memorable country bumpkins: the domineering ignoramus, Mrs Prostakova* (a Russian Mrs Malaprop) and her loutish son, Mitrofanushka—the minor. Fonvizin's thoughtful *Letters from France* (1778) bring out the strong undertow of national consciousness which developed simultaneously with (and in reaction to) the prevailing influx of French culture.

Towards the end of the reign, the young Karamzin introduced the pre-romantic cult of sensibility. In his enormously successful *Poor Lisa* (1792), a rustic idyll with a touch of 'gothic' melodrama, he waxed sentimental over the peasants, inviting his readers to consider them as innocent and childlike, objects of compassion rather than disdain. This idea was to find great favour in the nineteenth century. Karamzin also made important contributions to the literary language: in his own pure and elegant style, pruned of rough slavonicisms, he laid the standard for the age of Pushkin. His agreeable style was admirably exemplified in his urbane and cosmopolitan *Letters of a Russian Traveller* (1792). His sympathetic observations at the plight of aristocratic French *émigrés* presaged the profound spiritual revulsion which the Revolution evoked in him, and which, in the reign of Alexander I, was to make him a staunch apologist of conservative nationalism.

The writers of the age of Catherine, though polished and correct, were on the whole derivative and academic. A notable exception was the poet Derzhavin, who magnificently exemplified the potentialities of Russian verse. As poet-laureate, Derzhavin paid homage to Catherine's humanity and benevolence, good-humouredly apostrophizing her as *Felitsa;* and trumpeted forth the victories of Potyomkin and Suvorov in richly sonorous odes, rising to heights of pictorial splendour.

★ i.e. Simpleton.

In such martial odes as those on the storming of Ochakov and Izmail, he gave grandiloquent voice to the patriotism of the day. But Derzhavin was more than a court-poet: his philosophical elegiacs range majestically across the eternal verities of existence, relieved by delightful touches of mirth and wit. Derzhavin was a master of the Horatian sentiment, evocative singer of the pleasures of aristocratic life and their ephemerality. Though an imperial protégé and a professional civil-servant, he was uncorrupted by office, and on the contrary voiced his outspoken conviction of the duty of Catherine's viceroys to govern justly. With fearless integrity he dared to remind the Empress herself of her own mortality, in his pointed adaptation of Psalm 82, *To Rulers and Judges;* for which Catherine had him temporarily delivered to Sheshkovsky, on suspicion of 'jacobinism'.

The Russian Enlightenment

The Provincial Statute of 1775 gave rise to a quickening of cultural life in the countryside, hitherto a stagnant backwater, where the nobility was chiefly represented by women, old men and children, and culture by the priesthood. The summer season now saw an annual migration of nobles from the capitals to their country-seats. There gradually emerged in the provinces the style of gracious living to be made familiar by the novels of the nineteenth century. Country houses sprang up on the western model, with paintings, furniture, statues and carriages imported from the west, with spacious ornamental gardens and liveried servants. With the introduction of the social round—hunting parties, visits, balls, banquets and theatres, the upper crust of society began to mirror the education and polish of their western peers.

Gallomania, which had struck root in the reign of Elisabeth, continued to set the general tone of St Petersburg society. One noble astounded a French visitor with his detailed knowledge of Paris, gleaned entirely from books. Others, like Princess Dashkova and the young Karamzin, made the Grand Tour in person, returning with French clothes, books and turns of phrase with which to vary their Russian. Dimitry Golitsyn, Catherine's ambassador at Versailles, professed to be more fluent in French than in his native tongue. In the mansions, academies and *pensions* of St Petersburg, as well as at court, French was the accepted language of polite conversation. Many households had their *abbé* or *gouvernante* (especially when the French

Revolution caused large numbers to emigrate). Why gallomania should have exercised so marked a hold on Russian society is partly explained by a thoughtful Swiss observer: 'Under such a government as that of Russia', he wrote, 'which does not encourage interest in politics, home entertainment has become a great art. Splendour and exquisite comfort, luxury and aristocratic taste, abundance of food and refinement of table manner, lightness and frivolity of conversation, provide a compensation.'

The prevalence of this modish and indiscriminate gallomania, long since the butt of comedy and satire, also helps to explain the overall lack of seriousness towards the Enlightenment. The writings of the *philosophes*, witty and *risqué*, were received by the *beau monde* as avidly as all the other delights of France. Enlightenment catchwords were bandied across the drawing-rooms of St Petersburg. Several nobles, like Ivan Shuvalov, entered into direct correspondence with the *philosophes*. Others, like Princess Dashkova and Fonvizin, saw them in person, attending the Paris *salons* and making the pilgrimage to Voltaire at Ferney. Dimitry Golitsyn was an ardent patron of the Encyclopedists, and arranged for the publication of Helvetius' controversial *De l'homme*. Catherine herself helped to translate Marmontel's *Bélisaire*, officially banned in France; and received Diderot himself at St Petersburg in 1773. The works of the *philosophes*, in French or Russian, already graced the private libraries of the capital in the 1760s and 1770s, and were soon to be found in the provinces. The *Encyclopédie* itself appeared in Russian. Most popular of all were the works of Voltaire. 'They will produce citizens, geniuses, heroes!' exclaimed Catherine, voicing the hope that Russians would learn them by heart.

Yet the fundamental ideas of the *philosophes* did not strike home. Their books were treated as fashionable gimcracks rather than stimulants to thought and action. Voltaireanism, in particular, boiled down to little more than cheap jibes at religion, singularly misplaced in Russia: the servile Synod, after all, was hardly *l'infâme*. While affecting the most advanced humanitarianism at the *soirées* of St Petersburg, few nobles seriously contemplated surrendering one jot of their hard-won privileges. Nikita Panin and Shcherbatov, both admirers of western constitutionalism, denounced the *Nakaz* itself as revolutionary. '*Ce sont des axiomes à renverser des murailles!*' exclaimed Panin in horror. Princess Dashkova, bluestocking director of both the Academy of Sciences and the Russian Academy, the friend of Diderot and Voltaire, hotly defended serfdom as essential to the very survival of the nobility. Serfdom must at all costs be retained, as Shcherbatov revealingly put it— 'Whatever Natural Law may say'. To thinkers such as these, the Pugachov rebellion came as the crowning proof that, in Shcherbatov's words, 'the peasants have manifestly shown themselves unfit for freedom of any sort'. General Panin, freemason and constitutionalist, who, at the Legislative Commission, had even spoken in favour of alleviating serfdom, later excused his murderous suppression of the rebellion with the defiant cry: 'Their blood be upon me and my descendants!' Even the sensitive Karamzin thought only in terms of paternalism, not emancipation. Thus, Catherine's more radical aspirations fell on stony ground. As she complained to Diderot, it was one thing to express enlightened ideals on paper; she 'poor Empress,' had to deal with 'men's skins, which are ticklish and far more easily irritated'.

Catherine stood well to the left of the conservative constitutionalists. Her *Nakaz* was indeed remarkable for its open-mindedness and humanitarianism. She also strove to popularize her ideas through literature. She wrote several comedies and edited her own satirical periodical, *Omnium Gatherum*,* a rather anaemic attempt in the manner of Addison and Steele, to improve the manners of society through good-humoured raillery and chaff. Catherine appealed to common sense and moderation, poking inoffensive fun at country bumpkins, opinionated radicals and solemn freemasons.

Most serious humanitarian thought was often the result of a leavening of French ideas with German. For the nobility outside the court and the capital, German was commonly the first foreign language. German influences were strong at Moscow University and many Russians studied in Germany (for example, Lomonosov at Marburg, and Radishchev at Leipzig), then imbued with the ideas of Leibniz and Wolff. The essence of the *Aufklärung* that filtered back into Russia was its moral intensity, its emphasis on natural law as a source of duty rather than privilege, and its insistence on man's social role, his responsibility both to the state and to society as a whole. This pietism, moral earnestness and emotional commitment is reflected in the writings of Novikov and Radishchev.

In his satirical journals, *The Drone* and *The Painter*, Novikov followed a familiar pattern by attacking the St Petersburg fop and the rustic boor. But to him, gallomania was an object of reproach rather than ridicule,

* Vsyakaya Vsyachina.

since it was symptomatic of a basic spiritual emptiness and lack of social conscience, which made the noble indifferent to his fellow-man, the serf. Here, Novikov trod on controversial ground, and his journals were suppressed on the eve of the Pugachov rebellion. In the 1780s, he turned to educational propaganda. Under his editorship, Moscow University put out almost a thousand titles, mainly popularizations of the *philosophes* or handbooks on history, literature and the arts. Many had masonic or pietistic overtones. Catherine, offended by his implied criticism of her rule and his efforts to mobilize an independent public opinion, professed to find his activities subversive. In 1789, she ordered the closure of his press and the destruction of its publications. Three years later, she had Novikov incarcerated without trial in Schlüsselburg, whence he emerged after her death, utterly broken in health and spirit.

Freemasonry, which had begun in the reigns of Anna and Elisabeth as a somewhat disreputable social diversion, re-emerged in the 1770s and 1780s as the philosophy of religiously-inclined conservatives, who shunned the superficiality of Russian Voltaireanism, yet felt too emancipated to return to Orthodoxy. Chiefly Martinist and Rosicrucean, they held that reason alone, without spiritual regeneration, was sterile and ultimately dehumanizing. While experiencing strong feelings of guilt about serfdom, they abhorred political radicalism, favouring gradual social progress through philanthropic propaganda and good works. A much-respected mason was Schwartz, German-born professor of philosophy at Moscow University, who helped to finance Novikov's educational publications and organized charitable collections and famine relief. The Masons were particularly hard hit by the backlash of the French Revolution. Their secret rituals and foreign affiliations aroused Catherine's suspicions; and their lodges were closed down as nests of subversion.

The most intense and anguished cry of protest was raised by Radishchev, the 'Father of the Russian *Intelligentsia*', whose *Journey from St Petersburg to Moscow* aroused a furore on its appearance in 1790. In the form of a travelogue, Radishchev remorselessly stripped away the mantle of enlightened absolutism to uncover the glaring evils at the core of Catherine's Russia. 'I looked about me,' he wrote, 'my heart was lacerated by the sufferings of mankind.' With high emotion, he evoked the bitter realities of serfdom: the burdens of *corvée* and quitrent, the arbitrary humiliations, knoutings and forced marriages, the heartbreak of the serf auction—and the indifference of officialdom. To

Catherine's claim that her sole desire was the happiness of her subjects, Radishchev questioned the happiness of a society in which 'a hundred citizens, puffed up with pride, welter in opulence, while thousands have no assurance of food or shelter'. The publication of the *Journey*, coinciding with the onset of the French Revolution, touched Catherine to the quick. She denounced the book as 'manifestly revolutionary', and its author as 'a rebel worse than Pugachov'. All available copies of the *Journey* were seized and destroyed. Radishchev, after 'interrogation' by Sheshkovsky and summary trial, was condemned to death for treason, a sentence later commuted to exile in Siberia.

The confident, clear-headed optimism of the early part of the reign was clouding over. Catherine herself was not immune to a sense of unease and futility: 'Nothing but beginnings without ends,' she sighed, looking back across the years. Novikov and Radishchev highlight a deepening alienation from the state among thinking men, and a critical, ambivalent attitude towards westernization. Of what use was westernization, if it merely served, in Sumarokov's words, to turn 'unpowdered men into powdered animals?' Some, like Fonvizin and Karamzin, disenchanted with gallomania and appalled by the French Revolution, turned to a new concern for things Russian and a rediscovery of the Muscovite heritage. The mythology of the 'Russian soul' was already in the making when Fonvizin, in his *Letters from France*, argued that not only was Russia equal to the west; but in a certain sense, superior. Precisely because of her late start, she could avoid the corruptions of the west, inspired by the spiritual simplicity and deeper capacity for humanity which Fonvizin ascribed to the Russian character. In his claim that '*nous commençons et ils finissent*' was sounded the first note of messianic nationalism.

For those who contended that westernization had been acquired at the price of humanity and decency, it was natural to hold Peter I responsible. Yet, as Shcherbatov observed, reaching to the heart of the issue, without Peter, Russia would still be plunged in ignorance and obscurity. He reminded critics of autocracy that it was from 'that despotism that they received the very enlightenment wherewith to censure that despotism!' As to those who now spurned the cultural influence of France, he pointedly observed: '*On devait aimer sa nourrice*'. The debate between 'slavophils' and 'westerners' was already in the making.

For many who pondered Russia's past and contemplated her future, the eighteenth century, 'century of madness and wisdom', in Radishchev's words, closed in doubt, anguished heartsearchings or a hopeless stoicism. Shcherbatov's only answer was to pray for 'a better reign'. Radishchev, dogged by a relentless sense of guilt towards the people and despair with the state, took his life.

Conclusion—Catherine's legacy

Catherine's Russia was one of Europe's leading land powers and an active arbiter in western affairs. Henceforth, few issues of importance could be settled without her participation. This fact alone may be reckoned among the most fateful legacies of the reign. Russia now inherited a momentous international role, which it proved well-nigh impossible to shun even if she wished to. Retreats into neutrality seldom lasted. Within two years of Catherine's death, Russia began her energetic involvement in the long struggle against Revolutionary and Napoleonic France. Her foreign policy was characterized on the one hand by a continuing expansionism, particularly at the expense of Turkey, and on the other by the emergence of a markedly hostile attitude towards revolutionary and liberal developments in the west. While Catherine declared that one could not crush ideologies by cannon fire, she was preparing to do just that with regard to the French Revolution. Russia's future role as 'gendarme of Europe' already loomed on the horizon. In terms of military power and the political influence that went with it, Russia was undeniably a part of Europe.

Culturally, too, the upper crust of St Petersburg society was completely westernized. The polish and urbanity which had delighted Voltaire in his Russian visitors of the 1770s, was taken for granted by the close of the century. The provinces too began for the first time to share part of the lustre of the capital. In science, literature, the fine arts and even music, Russia was emerging from her foreign tutelage, and could boast the beginnings of an independent culture, nourished and enriched, but no longer stifled, by foreign influences. Outside the court, after all, Russian remained the first language of the educated; and while Russian literature could not yet vie with that of France, England or Germany, the appearance of a Lomonosov or a Derzhavin presaged its unique contribution in the next century.

In other respects, however, Russia's path diverged radically from that of the west. The political system which Catherine bequeathed to her successors was in all essentials the same military and bureaucratic leviathan-state which she inherited from Peter I. It was capable of maintaining Russia's Great Power status well into the nineteenth century; but it was too rigid, cumbersome and inflexible to keep pace with the crucial underlying processes which even in Catherine's day were already transforming the economic, social and political structure of the west. The Industrial and Democratic Revolutions found Russia comparatively unreceptive, or provoked a hostile, conservative reaction. Europe changed, but Russia marked time, and failed to make those readjustments without which her Great Power status could have no truly lasting basis. Why was the problem of readjustment so peculiarly intractable?

Other considerations apart, nature and geography alone presented Russia with obstacles of a kind unknown further west. While her population almost trebled in the course of the century (and all but doubled in Catherine's reign alone) to a total of nearly forty million, the means to sustain this huge increase did not lie near at hand. By 1800, the traditional heart of European Russia, the centre and north, low in fertility, were no longer even self-supporting. Only the acquisition of the remote southern provinces enabled Russia to support the population increase. Again, her main industrial base still lay in the Urals, a thousand miles from traditional centres of government and civilization. Both agriculture and industry posed extraordinary problems of transport, administration, labour and finance. The sheer effort needed to overcome such handicaps was bound to hinder Russia's ability to keep pace with western states in the throes of industrial and social change. Such problems, moreover, seemed to demand the unique organizational capacity, the unmatched authority and the unlimited political power which the leviathan-state alone could provide.

Yet the social system on which the state depended was appallingly rigid. Serfdom, the basis of that system, was not only morally inequitable: in an epoch of revolutionary change in Europe, it was a dangerous anachronism, which was ultimately to hold Russia back, with disastrous consequences. Outside the nobility, which made up less than one percent of the population, social mobility barely existed. Not even the handful of successful industrial peasants from the factories at Ivanovo were permitted to buy their way out of serfdom and thus add to Russia's embryonic *bourgeoisie*. The social system which Catherine

I

bequeathed was well able to support the burden of the leviathan-state, but it failed entirely to spread that burden more evenly and efficiently. A wholly disproportionate amount of effort was expended, not on modernizing society, but on keeping it from disintegration, by the permanent and unrelenting suppression of the masses. Against them was concentrated the coercive power of the state in its various forms: the army, the church, the secret police, the statute-book and the knout. If the Russian peasant was to gain a reputation for long-suffering and docility, it was because, as the Pugachov rebellion showed, the price of resistance was atrociously high.

Effective reform could come only from an educated ruling class, prepared to introduce it. Leaving aside the question of how deeply education had permeated the nobility in general, one of the undeniable paradoxes of cultural westernization was that its recipients had largely ceased to think of the common man as a fellow human-being. What the ruling class desired above all was the indefinite prolongation of the *status quo*, and the enjoyment of those privileges—economic, social and cultural—which it had so recently and so hardly won. To the nobility as a whole, the gaining of political rights or representative institutions, in so far as they considered it at all, was irrelevant. Their interests and aspirations were bound up with the preservation of the existing order. True, individual autocrats might from time to time prove dispensable ('autocracy tempered by assassination' was one definition of Russia's constitutional history) but autocracy itself was not; and its authority and mystique had to be kept sacrosanct and beyond dispute. 'Autocracy', as Karamzin was to inform Alexander I, 'is the Palladium of Russia; on its integrity depends Russia's happiness.' Russia's Great Power status, her diplomatic and military triumphs, her cultural renaissance, were cited to justify a doctrine of social and political conservatism, which echoed the complacent insularity of Muscovy, and foreshadowed in many essentials, the future programme of 'official nationality'.

Criticism, even constructive criticism of the regime, came to be considered subversive and un-Russian, particularly after the French Revolution, which released powerful crosscurrents of conservatism in Russia. The humanitarian and democratic ideals of the Enlightenment—the Rights of Man, Liberty and Equality—became suspect, tarred with the brush of mob violence. For, while it was conceded that Pugachov had not indeed read the *philosophes*, it was felt that his programme and theirs came to much the same in the end. The recurrence of peasant disturbances at the time of the French Revolution lent weight to these suspicions. These, in turn, inspired the vicious suppression of Novikov and Radishchev, with its ritual accompaniment of witch-hunts, book-burnings, show-trials and all the paraphernalia of the police-state.

Catherine herself was perhaps as much a prisoner of the system as anyone. Her 'liberal' approach—the encouragement of tolerance, civility and relative openmindedness—could go only so far in a society based on institutionalized inequality and held together by naked force. Given a society of this kind, Russian politics, as the Pugachov revolt brought home to her, could not be those of mass consensus, compromise and the *juste milieu*. Genuine considerations of state as much as of personal security obliged Catherine to show an iron hand beneath her velvet glove by cracking down hard upon dissent. She faced the classic dilemma of the reformer *manqué*, forced to suppress expectations to which she herself had originally given rise.

Those who took the Enlightenment seriously and sought to apply its canons to Russia, were a small, rootless minority of 'conscience-stricken gentry', isolated from their class, remote from the masses they wished to serve, and facing an agonizing conflict of loyalties towards the state which had nurtured them. Catherine had deliberately fostered the growth of an *Intelligentsia*—the intellectual elite and moral conscience of the nation—and had allowed it to enjoy an unprecedented degree of freedom. With the repression of her later years, however, this *Intelligentsia* found itself increasingly alienated from the state and forced, almost inexorably, into the role of an unofficial opposition. It was not the least of Russia's tragedies that so many of her best and most original minds should be, almost by definition, 'agin the government'. It was inevitable, however, that they should question the justice of a leviathan-state which continued to embody its own ends and, Moloch-like, to devour its own children.

Suggestions for Further Reading

Titles considered especially helpful to students are marked with an asterisk.

General Histories

A reliable general history of the period is P. Milioukov, C. Seignobos and L. Eisenmann, *Histoire de la Russie*,* vols. I and II (Paris, 1932–33), also available in an English translation by C. L. Markmann (New York, 1968). The relevant chapters of the *New Cambridge Modern History*,* vols VI, VII and VIII (London, 1970, 1957 and 1965) also provide sound overall coverage. M. T. Florinsky, *Russia. A history and an interpretation*,* vol. I (New York, 1953), is informative and lively, though markedly hostile. An up-to-date brief survey which takes account of recent scholarship and includes an excellent bibliography is M. Raeff, *Imperial Russia 1682–1825: the coming of age of modern Russia*ered* (New York, 1971). Overdrawn but stimulating is P. Dukes' brief attempt at a re-appraisal of Russia in the context of late 18th-century Europe, 'Russia and the eighteenth-century Revolution,'* *History*, 1971.

The classic 19th-century Russian authority, (though it reaches only to 1774) is S. M. Solov'yov, *Istoriya Rossii s drevneyshikh vremyon*, vols. VII to XV, available in a modern edition (Moscow 1962–6). The masterpiece of pre-1917 historical writing in Russia, is, however, V. O. Klyuchevsky, 'Kurs russkoy istorii', the appropriate sections of which appear in vols. IV and V of his *Sochineniya* (Moscow, 1958). An English translation by C. J. Hogarth (London, 1911–31) is, unfortunately, quite inadequate. Volume IV, however, appears in a reliable version by Liliana Archibald (New York, 1961). The fruits of marxist research are contained in three indispensable volumes of *Ocherki istorii SSSR. Period feodalizma:* (i) *Rossiya v pervoy chetverti XVIII veka;* (ii) *Rossiya vo vtoroy chetverti XVIII veka;* (iii) *Rossiya vo vtoroy polovine XVIII veka* (Moscow, 1954, 1957, 1956). The latest soviet collective work on the period, sound and concise, is *Istoriya SSSR s drevneyshikh vremyon do nashikh dney*, vol. III. *Prevrashchenie Rossii v velikuyu derzhavu* (Moscow, 1967). An older, thoughtful introduction to the century is A. Lyutsh, V. Zommer and A. Lipovsky, *Itogi XVIII veka v Rossii* (Moscow, 1910). An important collection of recent articles on a variety of aspects of 18th-century Russia is *Absolyutizm v Rossii (XVII–XVIIIvv)*. *Sbornik statey k 70-letiyu . . . B. B. Kafengauza* (Moscow, 1964).

Documents

The most recent collection is *A Source Book for Russian History from Early Times to 1917*, vol. II, *Peter the Great to Nicholas I*★ (ed.) G. Vernadsky *et al.* (Yale, 1972).

Documents of Catherine the Great. The Correspondence with Voltaire and the Nakaz of 1767★ (ed.) W. F. Reddaway (Cambridge, 1931) is a readily available collection, though unreliable with regard to texts and dates. For comprehensive excerpts in English, based on the definitive Besterman text, see *Voltaire and Catherine the Great: Selected Correspondence*★ (ed.) A. Lentin (ORP, Cambridge, 1973). The *Nakaz* is better read in the bilingual (French and Russian) edition by I. G. Bezgin (St Petersburg, 1893). The latest edition of *The Memoirs of Catherine the Great*★ is that of M. Budberg, translated by D. Maroger (London, 1955). This fascinating document ends, however, with Catherine's accession.

The following soviet collections are all useful: M. T. Belyavsky and N. I. Pavlenko (ed.) *Khrestomatiya po istorii SSSR: XVIII vek* (Moscow, 1963); M. T. Belyavsky (ed.) *Dvoryanskaya imperiya XVIII veka. Sbornik dokumentov* (Moscow, 1960); and *Pamyatniki russkogo prava*, vol. 8: *zakonodatel'nye akty Petra I* (Moscow, 1961).

Peter I

Two excellent short accounts are R. Portal, *Pierre le Grand*★ (Paris, 1961) and B. H. Sumner, *Peter the Great and the Emergence of Russia*★ (London, 1950). The definitive biography is R. Wittram's masterly *Peter I: Czar und Kaiser* (Göttingen, 1964). Klyuchevsky's classic study (vol. IV of his *Sochineniya*) is available in an English translation by Liliana Archibald under the title *Peter the Great*★ (New York, 1961). An important section on social history is, however, omitted. M. Raeff has collated varying historical verdicts in *Peter the Great: Reformer or Revolutionary?*★ (Boston, 1963). In Russian, N. Ustryalov, *Istoriya Petra*

Velikogo, 6 vols (St Petersburg, 1858–63) is still extremely useful. Special aspects of the reign are covered in S. Knyaz'kov, *Ocherki iz istorii Petra Velikogo i ego vremeni*, 2nd edition (St Petersburg, 1914).

Mid-Century Russia

An important account of the 1730 crisis by P. N. Milyukov is available in French, 'Les hommes d'en haut et la noblesse', in *Le mouvement intellectuel russe* (Paris, 1918). Compare W. Recke, 'Die Verfassungspläne der russischen Oligarchen im Jahre 1730 und die Thronbesteigung der Kaiserin Anna Ivanovna', *Zeitschrift für Osteuropäische Geschichte* II (1911), and H. Fleischhacker, '1730: das Nachspiel der petrinishchen Reform', *Jahrbücher fur Geschichte Osteuropas*, VI (1941). Documents on the crisis and a perceptive introduction appear in *Plans for political reform in imperial Russia** *1730–1905* (ed.) M. Raeff, (New Jersey, 1966), which also includes the constitutional scheme of N. I. Panin. Anna's reign is re-examined by A. Lipski, 'The "dark era" of Anna Ioannovna', in *Slavic and East European Review*, 15 (1956). A corrective to traditional views of mid-century Russia is provided by S. O. Schmidt, 'La politique interieure du tsarisme au milieu du XVIIIe siècle'* in *Annales* (I, 1966). On Peter III see M. Raeff, 'The domestic policies of Peter III and his overthrow', in *American Historical Review*, June 1970. In Russian the classic study of the 1730 crisis remains D. A. Korsakov, *Votsarenie imperatritsy Anny Ioannovny* (Kazan, 1880). The traditional interpretation has been most effectively challenged by G. A. Protasov, '"Konditsii" 1730g i ikh prodolzhenie' in *Uchonye zapiski tambovskogo pedagogicheskogo instituta*, XV (1957). Government under Anna is analysed in V. Stroev, *Bironovshchina i kabinet ministrov* (St Petersburg 1910). No scholarly study exists of the important reign of Elisabeth.

Catherine II

Catherine II also awaits a historian worthy of her. The best all-round biography is still A. Brückner's old-fashioned *Katharina die Zweite*,* (Berlin, 1883). Reliable short accounts are provided by O. Hoetzsch in the *Cambridge Modern History*,* vol. VI, 2nd edition, (London, 1925) and G. P. Gooch in *Catherine the Great and other studies** (London, 1954), a sympathetic synopsis. A more severe, but sound conspectus is that of R. Portal, 'Sous le masque du libéralisme'* in *Catherine de Russie*, (Collection Génies et Réalités, Paris, 1966). An invaluable collection of essays, including translations from important Russian sources, appears in *Catherine the Great: a profile*★ (ed.) M. Raeff (New York, 1972). For Catherine's relations with the *philosophes* and attitudes towards the Enlightenment, see Ch. De Larivière, *Catherine II et la Revolution française*★ (Paris, 1895). The finest short account of Catherine in Russian is that of Klyuchevsky, in lectures 75–81 of 'Kurs russkoy istorii', *Sochineniya*, vol. V (Moscow, 1958). Compare his excellent sketch, 'Imperatritsa Yekaterina II' (ibid, pp. 309–371).

Foreign Policy

An informative introduction is provided in the opening chapters of C. de Grunwald, *Trois siècles de diplomatie russe*★ (Paris, 1945). Two detailed studies of Russia's growing diplomatic involvement with the west are D. Gerhard, *England und der Aufsteig Russlands* (Berlin-Munich, 1933), and W. Mediger, *Russlands Weg nach Europa* (Brunswick, 1952). For the Seven Years' War, consult H. H. Kaplan, *Russia and the Outbreak of the Seven Years' War* (Berkeley, 1968), and L. Jay Oliva, *Misalliance: a study of French policy in Russia during the Seven Years' War*★ (New York, 1964). An older study, still informative, is L. Vandal, *Louis XV et Elisabeth de Russie*★ (Paris, 1900). On the partitions of Poland, see H. H. Kaplan, *The First Partition of Poland*★ (New York, 1962), and R. H. Lord, *The Second Partition of Poland*★ (Cambridge, Mass., 1915). On the eastern question, B. H. Sumner provides an excellent short introduction in *Peter the Great and the Ottoman Empire*★ (Oxford, 1949). For the connection between Polish and Turkish problems, A. Sorel, *The Eastern Question in the Eighteenth Century*,★ translated by F. C. Bramwell (London, 1898) is still a classic. For the most recent approach, consult the early chapters of M. S. Anderson, *The Eastern Question, 1774–1923*★ (London, 1966). An older classic is H. Übersberger, *Russlands Orientpolitik in den letzten zwei Jahrhunderten*, vol. I (Stuttgart, 1913). On the Crimea, see A. W. Fisher, *The Russian Annexation of the Crimea 1774–1783* (Cambridge, 1970). I. de Madariaga, *Britain, Russia and the Armed Neutrality of 1780*,★ (London, 1962) is a definitive study. For a negative contemporary view, see A. Lentin, 'Prince M.M. Shcherbatov as critic of Catherine II's foreign policy', *The Slavonic and East European Review*, (July, 1971).

Most soviet studies of foreign policy suffer from a strong national bias. Useful, nonetheless are L. A. Nikiforov, *Russko-angliyskiye otnosheniya pri Petre I* (Moscow, 1950) and *Vneshnyaya politika Rossii v posledniye gody severnoy voyny i nishtadsky mir* (Moscow, 1959); and E. I. Druzhinina, *Kyuchuk-kainardzhiysky mir 1774g* (Moscow, 1955).

Government and Institutions

E. Amburger, *Geschichte der Behördenorganisation von Peter dem Grossen bis 1917* (Leyden, 1966) provides exhaustive coverage. Useful is J. Hassell, 'Implementation of the Russian Table of Ranks during the eighteenth century', *Slavic Revue* (June 1970). G. Vernadsky, *Ocherki istorii prava russkogo gosudarstva. Period imperii* (Prague, 1924), is an excellent concise introduction to laws and institutions. A more recent guide is N. P. Eroshkin, *Istoriya gosudarstvennykh uchrezhdeniy dorevolyutsionnoy Rossii* (Moscow, 1968). On the Senate, consult the first two volumes of *Istoriya pravitel'stvuyushchego Senata za dvesti let 1711–1911* (St Petersburg, 1911) (ed.) A. N. Filippov, *et al*. The best study of administration remains A. D. Gradovsky, 'Vysshaya administratsiya Rossii XVIII st. i general-prokurory' in *Sochineniya*, vol. I (St Petersburg, 1899). On local government, see M. M. Bogoslovsky, *Oblastnaya reforma Petra Velikogo: provintsiya 1719–1727* (Moscow, 1902), and Y. V. Got'e, *Istoriya oblastnogo upravleniya ot Petra I do Ekateriny II*, 2 vols (Moscow, 1913, 1941). An interesting account of the 'westernization' of Russian absolutism under Peter I is V. I. Syromyatnikov, *'Regulyarnoe' gosudarstvo Petra I i ego ideologiya* (Moscow-Leningrad, 1943). Military history is exhaustively covered by L. G. Beskrovny, *Russkaga armiya i flot v XVIII veke: ocherki* (Moscow, 1958), and a recent collection of essays, *Voprosy voennoy istorii Rossii* (Moscow, 1969).

Social and Economic

For an introduction to the nobility, see the helpful chapter by M. Beloff in *The European Nobility in the Eighteenth Century*★, ed. M. Goodwin, 2nd edition (London, 1967). An extremely illuminating recent study, with many insights into intellectual history, is M. Raeff, *Origins of the Russian Intelligentsia. The 18th-century Russian Nobility*,★ (New York, 1966). P. Dukes surveys the materials of the Legislative Commission of 1767 in *Catherine the Great and the Russian Nobility*,★ (Cambridge, 1967). On the nobility and serfdom, J. Blum, *Lord and Peasant in Russia from the Ninth to the Nineteenth Century*★ (Princeton, 1961) is a reliable survey. For more detailed analyses, consult A. Kahan, 'The costs of "westernization" in Russia: the gentry and the economy in the eighteenth century,' *Slavic and East European Review*, XXV, 1 (March, 1966), and M. Confino, *Domaines et seigneurs en Russie vers la fin du 18e siècle* (Paris, 1963). On the peasants in the Urals, see R. Portal, *L'Oural au XVIIIe siècle* (Paris, 1951). On the Pugachov rebellion, highly recommendable is M. Raeff,

'Pugachev's rebellion,* in R. Forster and J. P. Greene (eds), *Preconditions of Revolution in Early Modern Europe* (Baltimore, 1970), and J. T. Alexander's informative *Autocratic Politics in a National Crisis: the Imperial Russian Government and Pugachev's Revolt** (Indiana U.P., 1969).

The two classic Russian studies of the nobility are A. Romanovich-Slavatinsky, *Dvoryanstvo v Rossii ot nachala XVIII veka do otmeny krepostnogo prava*, 2nd edition (Kiev, 1912), and S. A. Korf, *Dvoryanstvo i ego soslovnoe upravlenie za stoletie 1762–1855* (St Petersburg, 1906); to which should be added N. D. Chechulin, *Russkoe provintsial'noe obshchestvo vo vtoroy polovine XVIII veka* (St Petersburg, 1889). On the peasantry, the classic authority by V. I. Semevsky, *Krest'yane v tsarstvovanie imperatritsy Yekateriny II* (St Petersburg, 1881–1901), has been expanded, but not superseded by more recent monographs, notably P. K. Alafirenko, *Krest'yanskoe dvizhenie i krest'yansky vopros v Rossii v 30–50gg. XVIIIv* (Moscow, 1957) and V. V. Mavrodin, *Krest'yanskaya voina v Rossii 1773–1775 godakh: vosstanie Pugachova* (Leningrad, 1961–6). On the neglected topic of the town dwellers, consult A. A. Kizevetter, *Russkaya obshchina v Rossii XVIIIst* (Moscow, 1903).

A. Baykov provides some thoughtful rethinking about Russia's economic backwardness in 'The economic development of Russia',* *Economic history revue*, 2nd series, vii, 2 (1954). A soviet authority on economic development, available in English, is P. I. Lyashchenko, *History of the National Economy of Russia** (New York, 1949). Still useful, especially on the peasant question, is J. Mavor, *An economic history of Russia*,* 2 vols.; 2nd edition (London, 1925). On industry, a clear outline is provided in the early chapters of W. L. Blackwell, *The Beginnings of Russian Industrialization 1800–1860.** There is a sound account of trade with the west in W. Kirchner, *Commercial Relations Between Russia and Europe 1400–1800: Collected Essays* (London, 1967). S. Blanc gives an excellent summary of mercantilism under Peter I in 'A propos de la politique économique de Pierre le Grand', in *Cahiers du monde russe et soviétique*, vol. III, (Paris, 1962), while there are stimulating insights in A. Gerschenkron, *Europe in the Russian Mirror* (Cambridge, 1970). For the mid-century period, see A. Kahan, 'Continuity in economic activity and policy during the post-petrine period in Russia', *Journal of Economic History*, 25 (1965).

Available population statistics are supplied in V. M. Kabuzan, *Narodonaselenie Rossii v XVIII—pervoy polovine XIXv* (Moscow, 1963). P. N. Milyukov's critical indictment of the economic and social consequences of Peter I's reforms in *Gosudarstvennoe khozyaistvo Rossii v per-*

voy chetverti XVIII st. i reforma Petra Velikogo (St Petersburg, 1905) is challenged, not altogether convincingly, by B. B. Kafengauz, *Ocherki vnutrennogo rynka Rossii pervoy poloviny XVIII veka* (Moscow, 1958). Of the many soviet studies of industrialization, especially helpful are N. I. Pavlenko, *Istoriya metallurgii v Rossii XVIII veka* (Moscow, 1962), and P. G. Lyubomirov, *Ocherki po istorii russkoy promyshlennosti* (Moscow, 1947). On trade, see I. M. Kulisher, *Istoriya russkoy torgovli do XIX-go veka vklyuchitel'no* (Petrograd, 1923).

Education, Thought and Culture

On the neglected topic of the Church's contribution to education, see G. Bissonnette, 'Peter the Great and the Church as an educational institution', in *Essays in Honour of G. T. Robinson* (Leyden, 1963). On the Church generally, see I. Smolitsch, *Geschichte der russischen Kirche*, vol. I (Leyden, 1964). J. Cracraft had produced an excellent study of the Church under Peter I, *The Church Reform of Peter the Great*★ (London, 1971). An interesting probe into old and new concepts of religion and kingship is M. Cherniavsky, *Tsar and people*, (Yale, 1961). The theme of reactions to westernization is thoughtfully discussed in H. Rogger, *National Consciousness in 18th-century Russia*★ (New York, 1966) and by R. Pipes in the introduction to his edition of *Karamzin's Memoir on Ancient and Modern Russia*,★ 2nd edition, (New York, 1966). A. Vucinich, *Science in Russian culture. A history to 1860*★ (London, 1965), is extremely informative. B. N. Menshutin's biography of Lomonosov (1911) is available in English. On the Enlightenment in Russia, consult H. Jablonowski, 'Die geistige Bewegung in Russland in der 2 Halfte des 18 Jahrhunderts' in *Commission internationale des études slaves: ricerche slavistiche* (Upsala, 1960). Radishchev's *A journey from St Petersburg to Moscow*★ (ed.) R. Thaler appears in an English version by L. Wiener (Cambridge, Mass., 1968). There are two excellent biographies of Radishchev: D. M. Lang, *The First Russian Radical. Alexander Radishchev*★ (London, 1959) and A. McConnell, *A Russian 'philosophe:' Alexander Radishchev*★ (The Hague, 1964). For Shcherbatov, see *Prince M. M. Shcherbatov. On the Corruption of Morals in Russia*★ (Cambridge, 1969). On literature, H. B. Segel provides a comprehensive selection in translation with a good introduction in *The Literature of Eighteenth-Century Russia. A History and an Anthology*,★ 2 vols (New York, 1967). For social thought and selections in English from Shcherbatov, Novikov, Fonvizin and Karamzin, see *Russian Intellectual History. An Anthology*,★

(ed) M. Raeff (New York, 1966). Karamzin's *Letters of a Russian traveller* are available in an English translation by Florence Jones (New York, 1957).

A sound Russian study of the church is A. V. Kartashov, *Ocherki po istorii russkoy tserkvi*, vol. II (Paris, 1959). On education, M. I. Demkov, *Istoriya russkoy pedagogiki*, Part II (St Petersburg, 1897) is still very useful. *Feofana Prokopovicha i ee zapadnoevropeyskiye istochniki* (Yur'ev, 1915) is given in G. P. Plekhanov, *Istoriya russkoy obshchestvennoy mysli*, 3 vols (Moscow, 1918). The classic study of the westernization of culture under Peter I, P. Pekarsky, *Nauka i literatura v Rossii pri Petre Velikom* (St Petersburg, 1862) has not been superseded. G. Gur'vich, *Pravda voli monarshey Feofana Prokopovicha i ee zapadnoevropeyskiye istochniki* (Yur'ev, 1915) is rewarding reading on the theory of absolutism under Peter I. Another useful older classic for the first half of the century, is N. A. Popov, *Tatishchev i ego vremya* (Moscow, 1861). For a guide to the effects of the Enlightenment, see V. Tukalevsky, 'Filosofskiye napravleniya v Rossii vo vtoroy polovine XVIII veka' in *Zhurnal ministerstva narodnogo prosveshchemiya* (May, 1891). The influence of Voltaire is briefly outlined in D. D. Yazykov, *Vol'ter v russkoy literature* (Moscow, 1902). A lucid introduction to Russian freemasonry is contained in *Masonstvo v ego proshlom i nastoyasashchem* (ed.) S. P. Mel'gunov and N. P. Sidorov (Moscow, 1914). For close analysis, consult A. N. Pypin, *Russkoe masonstvo: XVIII i pervaya chetvert' XIX v.* (Prague, 1916). V. Bogolyubov, *N. I. Novikov i ego vremya* (Moscow, 1916) is still the best biography of Novikov. Full of interest is M. M. Shtrange's *Russkoe obshchestvo i frantsuzskaya revolyutsiya 1789–94gg.* (Moscow, 1956).

On art, consult the appropriate chapters of G. H. Hamilton, *The Art and Architecture of Russia,*★ scholarly and readable. The classic work of reference in Russian is *Istoriya russkogo iskusstva* (ed) I. E. Grabar' *et al.*, vols. V–VII (Moscow, 1960–61). N. Kovalenskaya provides two reliable and well-illustrated studies, *Istoriya russkogo iskusstva XVIIIv* (Moscow, 1962) and *Russky klassitsism* (Moscow, 1964). Connections between art and literature are explored in K. V. Pigaryov, *Russkaya literatura i izobrazitel'noe iskusstvo* (Moscow, 1966). The little-known field of musical life is exhaustively covered in C. Aloys-Mooser's monumental *Annales de la musique et des musiciens en Russie au XVIIIe siècle*, 2 vols (Geneva, 1948–51).

Index

Aaland Islands, 11, 12, 61
Abo, 11, Treaty, of 63–4
Academy of Fine Arts, 75, 112
Academy of Sciences, 37, 73, 91, 113, 116,
    Commentarii of, 73
Administration, Bureaucracy, Government,
    14–19, 25, 29, 31, 42–3, 48, 51, 52, 55,
    56–9, 68, 70, 72, 74, 81, 82–3, 84, 85–
    88, 102, 121
Admiralty, see Colleges
Aegean, 95
Agriculture, 24–5, 70, 90, 91, 92, 103, 121
Alexander I, 114, 122
Alexander Palace, 112
Alexei, Czar, 5, 6
Alexei, Czarevich, 20–21, 42, 47, 48
Alphabet, civil, 37–8
Amsterdam, 7, 38
Anhalt-Zerbst, Zerbst, 56, 80
Anna, Empress, 50–3, 54, 58, 59, 63, 68, 69,
    71, 73, 75, 80, 106, 118
Archangel, 6, 18, 27–8
Armed Neutrality, League of, 98
Armenia, 12
Army, Armed Forces, 5, 8, 9, 10, 11, 12, 14,
    15–16, 17, 18, 19, 24, 25, 26, 30, 31,
    32–3, 34–5, 52, 57, 59, 62, 63, 64, 65,
    66–7, 71, 72, 75, 86, 88, 89, 90, 91, 93,
    94, 96, 97, 98, 101–2, 106, 107, 108,
    109, 122
Art, Architecture, 38–9, 75, 112–13, 122
Artillery Academy, 31, 37, 72
Assemblies, Decree concerning the, 39
Assignats, 89
Astrakhan, 9
Atlas of the Russian Empire, 73
Aufklärung, see German influences
Austria, 6, 13, 61–2, 63, 64, 65, 66, 67, 93, 94,
    95, 96, 97, 98, 103
Azov, 7, 11, 63

Azov, Sea of, 95

Balance of Power, 12, 13, 61, 67, 96
Balkans, 95, 96
Baltic, 3, 6, 7, 8, 11, 12, 27, 28, 37, 40, 89, 90
Baltic provinces, the, (Courland, Estonia,
    Ingria, Karelia, Livonia), 7, 9, 11, 13,
    27, 28, 61, 64, 71, 75, 88
Bank of the Nobility, 70, 101
Bar, Confederation at, 94
Baroque, 38–9, 75
Bashkiria, 32
Bashkirs, 9, 28, 71, 107
Bavarian Succession, War of, 98
Bayle, 79
Bazhonov, 112–13
Beccaria, 84
Belgrade, 96, Treaty of, 63
Belorussians, 98
Berlin, 64, 65, 67
Bernoulli, Daniel, 73
Bessarabia, 96
Bestuzhev, 54, 57, 61, 62, 64–6
Betsky, 110, 112
Black Sea, 3, 6, 7, 11, 37, 63, 90, 93, 95, 97,
    106
Blackstone, 86
Boileau, 74
Bourgeoisie, 91, 121
Boyars' Duma, 14
Brandenburg, 66
Britain, England, 11, 12, 27, 29, 36, 54, 60,
    62, 64, 65, 66, 90, 91, 96, 120
Brunswick, house of, 53, 54
Brunswick, Princess of, 53
Bucharest, 96
Buffon, 79
Bug, river, 95
Bühren, 51–2, 53, 63, 94

Cabinet of Ministers, 51, 53, 57
Cadet Corps, see Noble Land Cadet Corps
Calendar, Julian, 38
Cameron, 112
Cameron Gallery, 112
Caspian, 37, 62
Catherine I, 6, 48, 49, 53, 58
Catherine II, the Great, character and reign,
    79–83
  and Church, 83
  and Legislative Commission, 83–5
  and Secret Chancery, 85–6
  and provincial reform, 86–8
  and economy, 88–92
  and foreign policy, 93–8
  and the nobility, 99–102
  and peasants, 103–4, 106, 108–9
  and education, 111–12
  and culture, 112–15
  and Enlightenment, 79–80, 84, 110, 116
    Charter of the Nobility, 99–100
    Municipal Charter, 86, 87–8
    Nakaz, 84, 104, 116, 117
    Omnium Gatherum, 117
    Provincial Statute, 86–7, 88
Caucasus, 71
Censorship, 80, 85–6, 113
Chancelleries, 15, 16
Charles VI, of Austria, 20, 62
Charles XII, of Sweden, 8, 9, 10, 11, 12
Charter of the Nobility, 99–100
Chesme, Cape, 94
Chief Magistracy, 18, 19, 58
China, 62
Christians, in Ottoman Empire, 11, 95
Church, Orthodox, 4–5, 7, 20–23, 36, 37–8,
    40, 42, 43, 56, 58–9, 71, 72–3, 74, 81,
    83, 85, 105, 112, 118, 122
'Cipher-schools', 37, 72
Classicism, Pseudo-Classicism, 74, 112–15
Cloth Industry, 25, 26, 27, 70, 89–90
Colleges, Collegiate System, 15–16, 43, 57,
    82, 86–7
  Admiralty College, 15, 16, 25, 82
  College of Foreign Affairs, 15, 16, 82
  College of Justice, 15
  College of Manufacturers, 26
  College of Mines, 26
  College of War, 15, 16, 73, 82
  Spiritual College, see Holy Synod
Colonisation, 28, 71, 97, 106, 107
*Commission for the drawing-up of a new code of
    laws*, see Law
Communications, 26–27, 32, 33, 89, 91, 121

Constantine, Grand Duke, 96
Constantinople, 4, 11, 62, 96
Constitutionalism, 117, 122
Consumer Industries, 25, 60, 90, 91
Corruption, administrative, 16–17, 18, 102
Corvée, 33, 103, 104, 107, 118
Cossacks, 9, 54, 107, 108
Cottage Industries, 89–90
Courland, 12, 49, 50, 51, 52, 64, 94, 97
Crimea, 63, 88, 94, 95, 96, 97
Crimean Tartars, 6, 61, 63, 97
Culture, 40, 55, 73–76, 80, 112–16, 120
Czarskoe Selo, 75, 112

Danube, 94, 95, 96, 106
Danzig, 62
Dashkova, Princess, 116
Debt, national, 59, 89
Decembrist Movement, 111
Demidovs, 26
Denmark, 7, 10, 12, 56, 62, 90
Derzhavin, 114–15, 120
    Felitsa, 114
    To Rulers and Judges, 115
Descartes, 3
Dictionary, first Russian, 113
Diderot, 80, 86, 116, 117
'Diplomatic Revolution', the, 65
Dissidents, Polish, 94
Dnieper, 95
Dniester, 96, 97
Dolgorukys, 48–51, 52, 101
Dresden, 75
Duma, municipal, 87
Dvina, river, 95

East Prussia, 64, 65, 66, 75
Economy, 19, 24–28, 55, 59–60, 88–92, 121
Education, 14, 22, 30, 36–7, 51, 68–9, 72–3,
    80, 87, 99, 100, 110–12, 122
Elbe, 12
Elisabeth, Empress, 50, 53–55, 56, 64, 65,
    66, 67, 69, 71, 73, 75, 79, 81, 89, 92, 105,
    106, 115, 118
Encyclopédie, 80, 116
Encyclopedists, 79, 80, 111, 116
Engineering Academy, 31, 37, 72
Enlightenment, 55, 76, 79–80, 81, 83, 84, 85,
    103, 116–17, 122, 123
Entail Law, 32, 68, 69
Estonia, 11, 12
Euler, Leonhard, 73
Exports, 27–8, 60, 89, 90, 91, 92

Falconnet, 81
Farquharson, 37, 38
Favourites, 48, 49, 51, 53, 54, 55, 68, 80, 82, 83, 106
Ferney, 116
Filaret, Patriarch, 5
Finance, 14, 15, 16, 19, 26, 52, 57, 59, 88–9, 91, 121
Finland, 11, 63
Finland, Gulf of, 9
Finns, 28
Fiskals, 16, 17, 43
Fokshany, 95
Fontenelle, 74
 Entretiens sur la pluralité des mondes, 74
Fonvizin, 114, 116, 119
 Brigadier, the, 114
 Letters from France, 114, 119
 Minor, the, 114
Foundlings' Homes, 110
France, 11, 12, 13, 36, 39, 40, 53, 61, 62, 63, 64, 65, 66, 67, 84, 90, 91, 93, 96, 97, 98, 102, 109, 111, 119, 120
Frankfurt-on-Oder, 66
Frederick II, of Prussia, 56, 64–7, 93, 94, 95
Frederick-William I, of Prussia, 42
Free Economic Society, 91, 103, 105
Freemasonry, 75, 86, 117, 118
French influences, 55, 64, 75–6, 79–80, 85–6, 115–16, 117, 119
French Revolution, 80, 81, 85, 97, 98, 109, 115–16, 118, 119, 120, 122, 123
Fyodor, Czar, 6

Garrison schools, 72, 112
'Gendarme of Europe', 120
Generalitet, 30, 49, 82, 84, 109
General Regulation, 16, 31
George I, of England, 12, 27
Georgia, 12
German influences, 51–3, 73, 117
'German Quarter', 5, 6, 7
Germany, 12, 15, 36, 98, 117, 120
Golitsyn, Dimitry, 115, 116
Golitsyns, 30, 48–50, 52, 101
Governor, Governor-General, Viceroy, 82, 86, 87, 88, 99, 100, 102, 115
Great Power Status, 7, 13, 24, 32, 40, 47, 61, 62, 93, 98, 120, 121, 122
'Greek Empire', project of, 96
Gross-Jägersdorf, 65, 66
Grotius, 42, 43
Guards, the, (Imperial Guards Regiments), 15, 31, 47–8, 49, 50, 51, 53, 54, 56, 68, 80, 81, 84, 85, 102
Gubernii, 17, 86, 109
'Guilds', 87

Habsburgs, 20, 62, 95
Hango, Cape, 11, 24
Hanover, 12, 64
Hanseatic League, 28
Helvétius, 116
 De l'homme, 116
Hobbes, 42, 43
Holland, 11, 29, 36, 38, 40, 89, 90
Holstein, Holstein-Gottorp, 12, 56
'Holy Russia', 4
Holy Synod, 21–2, 83, 116
Honourable Mirror of Youth, the, 39–40, 75
Horse Guards, see Guards, 31
Huygens, 38
 Cosmotheros, 38

Imperial Council, 82, 83, 86, 96
Imperial title, 13, 63
Imports, 25, 27, 52, 59, 60, 75, 90, 91
Industry, 5, 8, 14, 15, 19, 22, 25–6, 27, 28, 29, 32, 33, 52, 55, 59–60, 70, 71, 87, 89–92, 99, 107, 121
Inflation, 89, 102
Ingria, 11, 12
Intelligentsia, 118, 123
Iron Industry, 9, 24, 25–6, 27, 51, 59–60, 70, 89, 90, 92
Isolationism, 3, 4, 5, 7, 21, 36, 43, 122
Italy, 22, 36, 89
Ivan IV, the Terrible, 4, 13, 42, 43, 98
Ivan VI, 53, 54, 80, 85
Ivanovo, 90, 121
Izmail, 96, 115
Izmailovsky Regiment, see Guards, 51

Jassy, Treaty of, 96
Jesuits, 4, 22
Joseph II, of Austria, 80, 96, 111
Junkers, 31, 101
Justice, administration of, 15, 19–21, 52, 57, 83, 87, 88, 99, 100, 108–09

Kabardia, 95
Kagul, 94
Kalmyks, 107
Kamchatka, 12
Kamerir, 17, 34
Kantemir, 50, 74, 76
Kapitan-ispravnik, 87

Karamzin, 114, 115, 117, 119, 122
  Letters of a Russian Traveller, 114
  Poor Lisa, 114
Karelia, 12, 25, 89, 107
Kazan, 83, 108
Kazan *guberniya*, 35, 86
Kerch, 95
Kheraskov, 114
  Rossiada, 114
Kherson, 97
Kiev, 4, 6, 22–28, 36, 73
Kirghiz, 107
Kolberg, 67
Komissar, 34
Konferents, 55, 57, 66
Königsberg, 65
Kosciuszko, 97
Kuban, river, 97
Kuchuk-kainardzhi, Treaty of, 95–6
Kunersdorf, 66–7
Kurile Islands, 12
Küstrin, 66
Kymmenegard, 64

Labour, 2, 6, 28, 29, 32, 33, 71, 89, 90, 91,
  107, 121
Ladoga, Lake, 27
Law, Legislation, Codification, 19–20, 42,
  52, 55, 57, 58, 80, 81, 83–5, 86, 87, 99,
  104, 106, 117, 122
Leibniz, 15, 16
Leipzig, 111, 117
Lesnaya, 10
Leszczynsky, Stanislas, King of Poland, 62
Levitsky, 113
Levshin, Platon, 83
Literature, *belles-lettres*, 40, 74, 75, 76, 111,
  113–15, 116, 117, 119, 120
Livonia, 11, 12, 18, 51, 95, 97
Loans, foreign, 88–9
Locke, 110
Lomonosov, 55, 73, 74, 76, 110, 113, 120
  On Divine Majesty, 74
  Russian Grammar, 74
London, 74
Louis XIV, 3, 112

Magnitsky, 38, 73
  Arithmetic, 38, 73
Malorussia, 6, 88
*Manifesto concerning the Freedom of the
  Nobility*, 69, 71, 99
Marburg, 117
Maria-Theresa, of Austria, ftn. 62

Marmontel, 116
  Bélisaire, 116
Marshal of the Nobility, 87, 100–101
Mazepa, 10, 28
Mecklenburg, 12
Mediterranean, 95
Menshikov, 10, 16, 18, 26, 30, 35, 39, 48–9
Merchants, Townsfolk, 18–19, 20, 26, 28–9,
  39, 85, 87, 90, 91
Michael, Czar, 5, 6
Military Statute, 19, 42, 106
Mining Institute, 91
Minsk, 97
Moldavia, Moldavia-Wallachia, 11, 94, 95,
  96
Monasteries, 22, 83
Montesquieu, 79, 80, 84
Monthly Articles, 73–4
Mordvins, 71
Moscow, 3, 4, 5, 7, 8, 19, 25, 26, 30, 36, 38,
  49, 50, 52, 73, 82, 83, 84, 85, 88, 89, 107,
  108, 112, 113
Moscow *guberniya*, 18, 89, 106
Moscow News (I), 40
Moscow News (II), 73
Moscow University, 73, 74, 113, 117, 118
Mstislavl, 95
Municipal Charter, 86, 87–8
Münnich, 51, 53, 63, 72
Muscovy, 4, 6, 7, 13, 15, 24, 29, 39, 43, 122
Music, Opera, Ballet, 75, 110, 112, 113, 120

Nakaz, 84, 104, 116, 117
Narva, 8, 9, 14, 24, 25, 28
National Consciousness, 74, 101, 113–15,
  119, 120, 122
Natural Law, 84, 117
Naval Academy, 31, 37, 72
Navy, Fleet, 7, 9, 11, 17, 20, 25, 27, 31, 32,
  33, 57, 67, 89, 94–5, 96, 98
Neva, River, 9, 27, 33, 38
Nikolaev, 97
Nikon, Patriarch, 5
Nobility, 20, 21, 26, 27, 28, 29–32, 33–34, 36,
  39, 40, 43, 48–9, 50, 51, 53, 56–7, 58,
  68–70, 71, 72, 74–6, 83, 84, 85, 86, 87,
  99–102, 103, 104, 105, 107, 108, 109,
  110–11, 114, 115–17, 118, 120, 121–2,
  123
Noble Land Cadet Corps, 69, 72, 73, 75,
  102, 111–12
North-West Passage, 6
North Sea, 94
Novgorod, 22

Novikov, 86, 113, 117–18, 119, 123
  Drone, the, 118
  Painter, the, 118
Nystadt, Treaty of, 12, 61, 95

Ober-fiskal, 16–17, 31
Oberprokuror, of Synod, 21
'Oblique Tactic', 66
Ochakov, 96, 115
Odessa, 96
'Official Nationality', 122
Old Believers, 4–5, 20, 22, 29, 83, 107
Orenburg, 107
Ostermann, 51, 53, 54, 57, 59, 61–3

Palace-revolutions, 48, 56, 58, 80, 99
Panin, Nikita, 82, 96, 104, 116
Panin, Pyotr, 108, 109, 117
Paris, 74, 116
Parish schools, 37, 73, 112
Pashkov Mansion, 113
Patriarch, 4, 5, 21, 22
'Patriotic War' of 1812, 101
Paul, Czar, 30, 80, 85, 100
Pavlovsk, Palace of, 112
Peasants, 3, 9, 17, 18, 20, 24, 25, 26, 31, 32–5,
  39, 40, 52, 54, 59, 68, 69, 70–1, 75, 76,
  83, 84, 85, 86, 87, 88, 89, 90, 91, 99,
  100, 102–9, 111–12, 114, 117, 118–19,
  121–2
Pensions, 111
Periodicals, 73–4, 113
Penza, 108
Persia, 12, 61
Peter I, the Great,
  character and reign, 6–7, 8, 40–43
  and foreign policy, 7–13
  and Church, 7, 21–3, 37–8
  and opposition, 9, 20–21, 41
  and government, 15–20
  and economy, 24–8
  and nobility, 29–32
  and peasants, 32–5
  and education, 36–8
  and culture, 38–40
  death of, 48
    Decree concerning the Assemblies, 39
    General Regulation, 16, 31
    Military Statute, 19, 42, 106
Peter II, 48, 49, 50
Peter III, 56, 57, 66, 67, 69, 80, 83, 85, 93,
  106, 107
  *Manifesto concerning the Freedom of the
    Nobility,* 69, 71, 99

Peter and Paul fortress, 38–9
Peterhof, 75
Philosophes, 58, 80, 82, 86, 116, 118, 122
Podolia, 97
Poland, Poland-Saxony, 3, 5, 6, 7, 9, 10, 12
  61, 62, 64, 66, 71, 88, 93–4, 95, 97–8
Poll-tax, 34–5, 59, 89
Polotsk, 95
Poltava, 10, 11, 14, 24, 27
Polzunov, 91
Pomerania, 66
Poniatowski, Stanislas, King of Poland, 94
Population, 70, 103, 106, 121
Portsmouth, 7
Portugal, 90
Potyomkin, 80, 82, 86, 93, 96, 106, 113, 114
Pragmatic Sanction, 62
Preobrazhensky Prikaz, see Secret Chancery,
Preobrazhensky Regiment, see Guards, 31,
  54
'Pretenders', 71, 107
Prikazy, see Chancelleries
Procurator-General, 15, 16, 17, 31, 82, 83, 86
Prokopovich, Feofan, 22–3, 42, 50, 76
  Spiritual Regulation, 22, 37, 42
  True Law of the Monarch's Will, the, 42
Proviantmeister, 17
Provinces, 16, 17–19, 37, 57–8, 72, 82, 83, 84,
  86–8, 98, 108, 111, 115, 120
Provincial Statute, 86–7, 88
Provintsii, 17, 86
Prussia, 12, 56, 62, 64–7, 93, 94, 95, 97, 98,
  103
Pruth, River, 11, 14, 33, 63
Public Welfare Board, 87
Publishing, 38, 73, 113
Pugachov, Emel'yan, 81, 83, 85, 86, 88, 95,
  106, 107–9, 117, 118, 119, 122, 123
Pushkin, 74, 114

Quarenghi, 112
Quitrent, 33, 89, 103, 104, 107, 118

Radishchev, 86, 105, 117, 118–19, 120, 123
  Journey from St Petersburg to Moscow,
    118–19
Rastrelli the Elder, 39
Rastrelli the Younger, 75
Rebellion, Political Opposition, 4, 9, 17, 20,
  21, 22, 71, 83, 85, 86, 88, 106–9, 123
Rehnsköld, 10
Reval, 18
Rhine, 62
Riga, 8, 18, 28

Rikhman, 74
Rococco, 75, 112
Romanovs, 4, 12, 63
Rome, 4, 112
'Third Rome', 4
Romodanovsky, 20, 30
Rostov, 83, 85
Rousseau, 80, 110
    Emile, 80
Russian Academy, 113, 116
'Russian Soul', 119
Rymnik, 96

Saltykova, Dar'ya, 105
Saratov, 108
Saxony, Saxony-Poland, 7, 8, 10, 64, 65
Scandinavia, 15
Schism, the, 4
School of Mathematics and Navigation, 36-7
Schlüsselburg, 54, 85, 118
Schwartz, 118
Science, Scientific Spirit, 4, 22, 36, 37, 38, 73, 74, 80, 120
Sebastopol, 96, 97
Secret Chancery, 20, 21, 23, 30, 52, 53, 55, 58, 70, 85-6, 108, 122
Semipalatinsk, 12
Semyonovsky Regiment, see Guards, 31
Senate, 14-15, 16, 30, 43, 48-9, 55, 57, 82-3, 86
Sensibility, Cult of, 114
Serfdom, see Peasants
Sestroretsk, 25, 27
Seven Years' War, 55, 58, 65-7, 75, 81, 93
Shafirov, 11, 26, 30
Shcherbatov, 100, 104, 113, 116, 117, 119, 120
    History of Russia, 113
Sheremetev, Field Marshal, 10, 30
Sheremetev, Nikolai, 100
Sheshkovsky, 85, 86, 108, 115, 119
'*Shpitsrut*', 33
Shubin, 113
Shuvalov, Alexander, 55, 58, 85
Shuvalov, Ivan, 55, 73, 75, 116
Shuvalov, Pyotr, 54, 55-6, 58, 59, 70
Shuvalovs, 57, 59, 81
Siberia, 12, 19, 37, 49, 52, 54, 58, 59, 62, 70, 71, 88, 105
'Slavophils', 119
Smolensk, 6
Smol'ny Cathedral, 75
Smol'ny Institute, 110-11, 113

Sophia, Regent, 6
Spain, 13
Spanish Succession, War of, 11
Spiritual College, see Holy Synod
Spiritual Regulation, 22-3, 37, 42
Stanileshti, 11
Starov, 113
State, concept of, 23, 41-3, 47, 119, 121-3
State-service, 28, 29, 30-33, 34, 42-3, 47, 57, 68-9, 76, 99, 100, 101-2, 103, 107
State Loan Bank, 70, 101
Stockholm, 12, 61
St Petersburg, 9, 11, 18, 19, 24, 25, 26, 27, 28, 30, 31, 33, 37, 38-39, 43, 49, 51, 54, 58, 63, 64, 65, 74, 75, 82, 86, 88, 90, 91, 96, 97, 108, 110, 112, 113, 115, 116, 117, 120
St Petersburg News, 73, 104
Strel'tsy, 5, 20
Succession, problems of the, 20-21, 47-8, 56, 65-6, 67
Succession-law, 47, 48
Sumarokov, 73, 75, 76, 114, 119
    Busy Bee, 73
    Dimitry the Pretender, 114
    Khorev, 75
Supreme Privy Council, 49, 50, 51, 57, 80
Suvorov, 96, 97, 114
Sweden, 3, 5, 6, 7, 8, 9, 10, 11, 12, 13, 18, 27, 28, 40, 53, 60, 61, 62, 63-4, 65, 68, 96

Table of Ranks, 29, 31, 57, 70, 73, 87
Taganrog, 7, 11
Tartars, 28, 114, cf. Crimean Tartars
Tatishchev, 50, 76
Taurid Palace, 113
Taxation, 14, 15, 17, 18, 19, 26, 28, 32, 33, 34-5, 52, 59, 71, 83, 87, 89, 99, 100, 106
Technology, 6, 7, 9, 24, 26, 36, 38, 40-41, 89, 91
Theatre, 4, 75, 113, 114, 115
Tilsit, 65
'Time of Troubles,' 3, 4
Torture, judicial, 19-20, 21, 30, 33, 52-3, 58, 85, 86, 99, 100, 105, 108-9, 122
Towns, 18-19, 25, 29, 43, 83, 84, 87-88, 91, 108
Trade, 14, 15, 27-8, 57, 58, 59, 89, 90, 91-2, 99
Tressini, 38-9
Tsaritsyn, 108
Tula, 5, 25, 89
Turkey, 4, 5, 6, 7, 10, 11, 13, 53, 61, 62-3, 64, 85, 90, 94-7, 98, 120

Tver', 18

Ukraine, 4, 10, 25, 28, 32, 61, 88, 97, 103
Universities, 73, 111, 117
Ural, River, 107
Urals, 9, 24, 25, 26, 27, 28, 33, 60, 71, 89, 107, 121
Ushakov, 52, 58, 85

Val'dmeister, 17
Venice, 38
Versailles, 38, 39, 54, 112, 115
Viceroy, Governor-General, see Governor
Vienna, 20, 75, 95
Vilna, 95
Vladimir *guberniya*, 90
Voevoda, 17, 18, 34, 37, 57–8, 88
Volga, 27, 28, 71, 108
Volhynia, 97
Volkhov, 27
Voltaire, 55, 75, 79, 80, 81, 84, 86, 116, 118, 120

Zaïre, 75
Volynsky, 53, 76
Vyazemsky, 82, 85, 104
Vyborg, 11, 28, 64

Warsaw, 61, 62, 97
Watt, James, 91
Westernisation, 4, 5, 6, 7, 9, 13, 36, 38, 39, 40–41, 42–3, 55, 61, 74–6, 110–11, 115, 121, 122–3
'Westerners', 119
White Sea, 6
Winter Palace, 49, 54, 75, 82
Wolff, Christian, 37, 117

Yaguzhinsky, 15, 17, 30
Yekaterinoslav, 97
Yenikale, 95

Zorndorf, 66

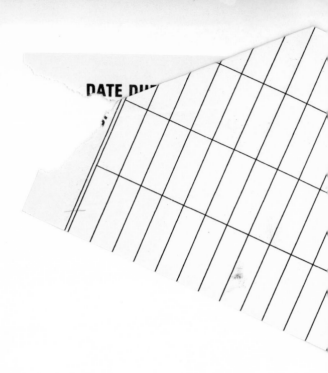

DATE DUE